THE
KONKANI LANGUAGE
AND
LITERATURE

THE
KONKANI LANGUAGE
AND
LITERATURE

J. GERSON DA CUNHA

GYAN

Published by

Gyan Publishing House
5, Ansari Road
Daryaganj, New Delhi-110002
Phone: 011-47034999, 9811692060
E-mail: books@gyanbooks.com

Distribution Network
gyanbooks.com
India, USA, Canada, UK, Australia, France

ISBN : 978-81-212-3669-0 (PB)
First Published, Bombay, 1881

2nd Impression 2020

Printed at: Gyan Press, Delhi.

The
Konkani Language and Literature
Author: J. Gerson Da Cunha

THE

KOṄKAṆÎ LANGUAGE AND LITERATURE.

BY

J. GERSON DA CUNHA,

M.R.C.S. AND L.M., ENG.; L.R.C.P., EDIN.;

Knight of the Order of St. Gregory the Great; Member of the Committee of Management of the Bombay Branch of the Royal Asiatic Society; Member of the Royal Asiatic Society of Great Britain and Ireland; Corresponding Member of the Royal Academy of Sciences of Lisbon; of the Oriental Academy of Florence; of the Academy of Science, Literature and Arts of Lyon; of the Arcadia of Rome; of the Adriatic Society of the Natural Sciences of Trieste; of the I. R. Zoological and Botanical Society of Vienna; Fellow of the Geographical Society of Italy, and of that of Lisbon; Fellow of the University of Bombay, &c.

For the Bombay Gazetteer.

Bombay:

PRINTED AT THE

GOVERNMENT CENTRAL PRESS.

1881.

THE KOṄKAṆÎ LANGUAGE AND LITERATURE.

I.

THE Koṅkaṇî language is spoken throughout that narrow strip of land which is bounded on the north by Malvâṇ, on the south by Karwâr, on the east by the Western Ghâṭs, and on the west by the Arabian sea. The people that speak this language may be estimated at about a million and a half, but the absence of a trustworthy census requires this estimate to be considered as a mere approximation.

Although the limits here assigned to Koṅkaṇî are the natural boundaries of a linguistic region, there are thousands of the natives of the Koṅkaṇ settled elsewhere, still speaking their mother-tongue, which makes its geographical distribution overstep the above lines of demarcation. Besides a small community of the Śeṇvîs and nearly twenty-five thousand Goanese Christians resident in Bombay, there are colonies of the Koṅkaṇîs in Honâvar and Mangalore, all of whom continue to speak this language. Some of the Koṅkaṇî Brâhmaṇs are settled as far south as Cochin, where they speak and write in their idiom. A proof of this assertion, some two centuries old, may be found in a testimonial in this language, in Devanâgarî characters, published in Van Rheede's *Hortus Indicus Malabaricus*, Amsterdam edition of 1678, above the signature of three learned Brâhmaṇs. It is also in this language that almost all the plants described in that work are named, although the author calls it *lingua bramanica*. Then Mr. Day, in his *Land of the Permauls*, p. 208, writes: "They (the Koṅkaṇî Brâhmaṇs) are nearly twice as numerous as the Nâmburî Brâhmaṇs. They are not allowed to officiate in the temples of the latter, or the Nâmburîs in theirs, while many deny them the title of Brâhmaṇs, to which they are undoubtedly entitled. They came originally from the Koṅkaṇ, from which their name is derived." The Koṅkaṇî Brâhmaṇs must not, however, be confounded with the Koṅkaṇasth Brâhmaṇs, which is another sub-division of Brâhmaṇs, generally known by the name of Chitpâvans. The extent of the country, or area, over which the Koṅkaṇî is spoken, is nearly 7000 square miles. It is spoken then not only in Malvâṇ; in about two-thirds of the district of Kuḍâl or Sâvantvâḍi, where the Koṅkaṇî assumes the dialectic form and name of Kuḍâlî; in the whole of the Portuguese territory of Goa, where considerable phonetic and even structural difference of vocables is observed in each of the districts into which that country is divided, as far as Karwâr, about fifty-five miles to the south; in Honâvar and in Mangalore; but also in Bombay and in Cochin.

The name of Koṅkaṇî applied to this language seems to be of a comparatively recent origin. The word by itself ought to refer to the whole Koṅkaṇ, which is a rather extensive country. A well-known tradition among the natives of Western India ascribes the creation or reclamation from the sea of the whole of this tract of land to Paraśurâma, one of the *avatârs* or incarnations of Vishṇu; its extent being 100 *yojanas* or 800 miles in length, and three *yojanas*, or twenty-four miles in breadth. This country, which is known by the name of *Paraśurâma-kshetra*, has been divided into seven parts, the region where Koṅkaṇî is spoken being called Madhya-Koṅkaṇa or simply Koṅkaṇa. Now the boundaries of this division of 'the Paraśurâma's country' are said to be the Vaitâraṇî or Danturâ river on the north, and the Aligâ river on the south, the former close to Bassein, and the latter near Karwâr, the whole strip of land being placed between the Sahyâdri range on one side and the coast of the Arabian sea on the other.[1] It is now divided into the Northern and Southern Koṅkaṇs, the first commencing north-east of Bombay and extending as far as Ratnâgiri, more properly as far as Malvâṇ, and the second ending at Karwâr. The name of Koṅkaṇî ought therefore to be confined to the latter region; but that it is of a comparatively modern date is proved by the fact of the Portuguese missionaries, who wrote some of their works in this language in the sixteenth and seventeenth centuries, designating it indiscriminately *lingua canarim* or *canarina* or 'Kânarese language,' which is evidently a misnomer, and *lingua concana* or *cancanica*, now generally written *concani*, while others name it *lingua bramana*, or *bramana-goana*, or simply *goana*. Now it does not seem probable that there should have been such a series of denominations when the language had a primitive name of its own. But even if it had it, one does not now know what it was like.

Nor is this an appropriate appellation; for the word Koṅkaṇî has not unfrequently been a source of confusion, mistaking the dialect thus called of the Marâṭhî with the Koṅkaṇî proper. It is well-known that the Marâṭhî language has two principal dialects, the Deshî or Dakhaṇî, spoken in those parts of the Dakhaṇ which lie to the northward and eastward of Puna, and the Koṅkaṇî spoken throughout the Northern Koṅkaṇ, as far south as Malvâṇ or southern districts of the Ratnâgiri Collectorate.[2] It was in the latter dialect also that some of the Portuguese missionaries wrote their works on Christianity and a grammar of it in the seventeenth century, but, with a negligence or disregard for a correct philological nomenclature which has been noticed elsewhere, they called it *lingua canarina do norte*, or 'the Kânarese language of the north.'

A cursory glance at the works written in the Koṅkaṇî dialect of the Marâṭhî, and in the Koṅkaṇî proper, will manifest palpably enough the difference subsisting between the two. A description of the former is given by my friend Dr. Murray Mitchell, who says: "The language is neither more nor less than a debased Marâṭhî, with a considerable admixture of Gujarâtî and Hindustânî. It is very closely allied to the dialect spoken in the island of Sâlsette near

---

[1] Earlier writers, however, apply the name of Konkan to the whole of the Western Coast, from the Tâpti or even Narbudda to the Cape Comorin, calling it *S'ûrpâraka*, or winnowing-fan like, from its shape resembling a winnowing-fan or basket. *Vide* Sk. Dict. sub voce *s'ûrpa*, Mah. Kon. *sûp*, a basket, or fan for winnowing grain.

[2] Selections from the Records of the Bom. Gov. No. X. N. S. 1854. Major Auld's notes on Sâvantvâdi.

Bombay. In this part of Western India, the Roman Catholic religion made exceedingly little impression on the higher castes of Hindûs; the converts were almost exclusively from the poorer classes of cultivators and fishermen, and their dialect of Marâṭhî has apparently been adopted by their religious teachers without any effort being made to elevate or systematize it."[1] In another place the same distinguished writer in reference to the following remark by Mr. Beames: 'The Koṅkaṇî dialect differs not very strikingly from the Deshî, and some of its forms are considered as more in harmony with the general analogy of the language than those in use in the Dakhaṇ,'[2] says, "Mr. Beames speaks indeed of Koṅkaṇî, but he means only that form of Marâṭhî which is spoken below the Ghâṭs and which differs in a very slight degree, and in its inflections not at all, from the language as spoken above the Ghâṭs. But there is another dialect of Marâṭhî which might almost be reckoned an additional language differing from Marâṭhî nearly as much as Gujarâtî does; and this is known by the name of Koṅkaṇî. It extends from Goa to Honâvar."[3] Instead of calling Koṅkaṇî 'another dialect of Marâṭhî,' it would, perhaps, be more to the purpose to designate it a cognate language, or one allied to Marâṭhî.

The late Dr. Wilson is more explicit yet in claiming a separate linguistic existence for Koṅkaṇî. He writes: "In connexion with the Marâṭhî language it is proper to notice the kindred Koṅkaṇî, above alluded to. By this designation is not meant the very slight dialectic difference which exists between the language of the British Dakhaṇ and the corresponding country running between the slopes of the Ghâṭs and the Indian Ocean, forming the British Koṅkaṇ, but the language of the country commencing with the Goa territories and extending considerably to the south of Karwâr and even Honâvar. The speech of this district differs from Marâṭhî as much as the Gujarâtî differs from Marâṭhî. It is manifestly in the main formed, however, on the basis of the Sanskṛit, and compared with other vernacular dialects, throws some light on their formation from the Sanskṛit, and on some of their peculiar grammatical forms." And then, in confirmation of the above statements, adduces an example of the declension of a noun, and that of the conjugation of the present tense of the substantive verb, adding that they are illustrative of a subject which has excited but little attention.[4]

But the existence of Koṅkaṇî, as quite distinct from, though cognate with, Marâṭhî and other allied tongues of the Âryan group, and having an equally elaborate grammar of its own, appears to have attracted the attention of Orientalists some years before the above mentioned writers alluded to it. To Portuguese ecclesiastics it was known as early as the sixteenth century, although they appear to have been either ignorant of, or else indifferent to, its relations to other languages. In 1847 Mr. (now Sir W.) Elliot wrote: "A dialect of the Koṅkaṇî is spoken in all the tract north of

---

[1] J. B. B. R. As. Soc. vol. III. p. 136. This paper was read in January 1849.

[2] A Comparative Grammar of the Modern Âryan Languages, London 1872, vol. I. p. 104.

[3] The Indian Antiquary, Bombay 1875, vol. IV. p. 190.

[4] The Bombay Administration Report, 1872-73.

Sadâshivgaḍ, and Marâṭhî is the language of the mountains immediately above it." And the late eminent Indianist, C. Lassen,[1] following the authority of Ellis and Mackenzie, referred to it as a distinct member of the Indo-Âryan family of languages. In 1853 Sir E. Perry said, that the Koṅkaṇî appeared to him to be no other than Marâṭhî with a large infusion of Tulu and Kânarese words, but that the subject required a closer philological investigation than it had yet received, as he was informed by the Rev. H. Mögling, of Mangalore, that the Koṅkaṇî speaking Brâhmaṇs of that part of the coast, where the language is vernacular, consider it quite distinct from Marâṭhî, and that its southern limit is a village four miles north of Upi or Udapi, near Cundâpur (Kundâpura), where Tulu, or the language of Kânaḍa begins.[2] He then consulted on the subject the late Mr. Murphy, Chief Interpreter of the High Court, whose note he subjoins, stating that "an examination of the grammar of the Koṅkaṇî proves it to be decidedly that of the Marâṭhî language. The nouns and verbs are inflected in the same manner, with some slight modifications in the details. A general characteristic which it shares with Gujarâtî and Mârvârî, is the adoption of *o* as the masculine termination, instead of the *â*, used in Hindî and Marâṭhî . . . . The Koṅkaṇî explains some of the difficulties of the Marâṭhî : what are anomalies or defective in the latter are sometimes found normal and complete in the former. It bears the stamp of a peculiar Brâhmaṇical influence, many Sanskṛit words being in common popular use for natural objects which are not so, as far as I know, in any other part of India. These are pronounced purely by the S'eṇvîs, but by the common Christian population (natives of Goa), are corrupted. Thus the common terms for water, tree, and grass, are Sanskrit : pronounced by the S'eṇvîs *udak, vriksh, trin ;* by native Christians *udik, rukh, tan.*[3]" The latter pronunciation is current among the lower classes ; but of this more hereafter.

Among later writers on this subject, Messrs. Cust,[4] Beames,[5] and Hoernle,[6] distinguished scholars in the domain of Âryo-Indian linguistics, deserve special mention. Tempting though it is, I refrain from citing these distinguished writers' opinions, as a string of quotations, of which we have already a good number, renders the reading extremely tedious. I may, however, state in short, that all

---

[1] Indische Alterthumskunde, vol. I. p. 360.

[2] J. B. B. R. A. Soc. Bombay 1853, vol. IV. p. 300. [3] *Ibid.*

[4] A Sketch of the Modern Languages of the East Indies, London 1878, p. 59-60. Elsewhere Mr. Cust writes : "Dr. Gerson da Cunha is about to publish a grammar of Konkaṇî, which has been provisionally classed by me as a dialect of Marâṭhî, subject to correction, if need be, from so good an authority." J. R. A. Soc. London 1879, vol. XI. N. S. p. 63. Thanking very much for the kind appreciation, I regret that absolute want of leisure has hitherto prevented me from completing the work here alluded to.

[5] A Comparative Grammar of the Modern Âryan Languages, London 1879, vol. III. p. 532-254.

[6] Calcutta Review, 1878, vol. LXVI. p. 754. I have not yet received the Comparative Grammar of the Gaudian Languages by the same author recently published. [N.B.—Since writing this note, a copy of the work has reached me. I am glad that its perusal only confirms the opinions I have expressed above and elsewhere.]

of them are agreed in considering Koṅkaṇî, not as a distinct member of the Âryan group, but as a dialect of the Marâṭhi.

But now the question arises, how is one to distinguish a language from a dialect? These are two relative terms, simple in themselves, but giving room for considerable difference of opinion. It is not yet settled for instance, whether Hindî and Panjâbî are sister languages, independent members of the same Neo-Âryan or Gauḍian group, or only eastern and western dialects of one great language. A rough test for deciding the question is to know whether a Hindî-speaking person can understand, as fast as it is spoken or read, the Panjâbî. An Italian, for example, can understand all Italian dialects easily enough, whether Genoese, Tuscan or Piamontese; but with considerable difficulty, Portuguese or Spanish, the latter being independent languages of the same family or group of tongues. Having applied this test to Koṅkaṇî, it has been observed that a Marâṭhâ does not understand it as easily as he understands the dialects of Marâṭhî, such as Koṅkaṇî, Nâgpurî or Khândeshî, in relation to the Deshî or that spoken in and about Puna, which is the standard and dominant type of that language.

Again a dialect has not, as a rule, any sub-dialects; but Koṅkaṇî has three distinct dialects, viz., the northern generally known as Kuḍâlî, spoken in the district of Sâvantvâḍî; the middle Goadesî or Gomâṅtakî, spoken in the Goa territory, with considerable variations in words and sounds in the old and new conquests, as well as in the three provinces of the former, Ilhas, Bardez, and Sâlsette; and lastly the southern or that spoken by the Koṅkaṇî colony settled in Kânaḍa, in such places as Honâvar and Mangalore.

The above arguments are not, however, sufficient to claim a separate linguistic existence for Koṅkaṇî. A more scientific method to determine the exact relation of Koṅkaṇî to Marâṭhî is necessary, viz: difference in the ordinary terms of their vocabularies, and in their principal phonetic and morphological changes.

The following list of words in ordinary use among the Koṅkaṇâs, all of them derived from Sanskṛit, is scarcely known to the Marâṭhâs, whose equivalent terms, or words of similar meaning, are also appended for the sake of comparison. If any of these words are used by the Marâṭhâs, they must be so among the learned, being later Sanskṛitised importations, and not by the people.

Koṅkaṇî.	*Sanskṛit.*	*Marâṭhî.*
Ahum 'I'	Aham	Mî.
Parvó 'a pigeon'	Pâravâ	Kabutar (Pers. کبوتر).
Kîr 'a parrot'	Kîra	Popaṭ.
Bókem 'a crane'	Baka	Bagalâ.
Suném 'a dog'	Svân (*Zendicè* span)	Kutrâ.
Zang 'the thigh'	Zangâ	Mândî.
Póló 'the cheek'	Kapola	Gâl.
Kankon 'a bracelet'	Kaṅkaṇa	Bangaḍî.
Razu 'a cord'	Raṅzu	Dorî.[1]

[1] रज्जु (*razu*) is also a Marâthî word, but used in a sense different from that of the Konkanî.

And several more, the identity whereof with Sanskṛit can be easily verified, are not in use among the Marâṭhâs.

It is said that the Marâṭhî language is the nearest to Sanskṛit of all the vernacular languages of India, but as far as ordinary expressions in use are concerned, Koṅkaṇî may perhaps claim to be not only the southern-most, but also the more closely allied representative of the North-Indian or Âryan family of languages. Although Koṅkaṇî has many words in common with Marâṭhî, and is perhaps more influenced by it, from its close proximity, than by any of the neighbouring Drâviḍian languages of the coast, still there are words current among the Koṅkaṇâs, which cannot have been derived from Marâṭhî. The first personal pronoun for instance, *ahum*, is more closely related to the Gujarâtî *hum*, and Hindî *haum* than to the Marâṭhî *mî*, and is of direct descent from Sanskṛit *aham*. Then the verbs *poleum* 'to see,' *uloum* 'to speak,' *apoum* 'to call,' *vochum* 'to go,' and several others are derived from Sanskṛit, their equivalents in Marâṭhî in ordinary use being quite different. Then the expression *kitem* 'what' cannot have the least connexion with the Marâṭhî *kâya*, but is composed of two Sanskṛit words *kim* 'what,' and *tat* 'that.' Again, the adverbs *khim* 'where,' and *thim* 'there,' have nothing to do with the Marâṭhî *koṭem* and *tethem*, but are derived from the Sanskṛit *kutra* and *tatra*, through the intermediate Prâkṛit stage of *kahim* and *tahim*.

With regard to phonetics and grammatical variations of forms in Koṅkaṇî, for the purpose of distinguishing the latter from Marâthî, I need not adduce here more than one or two examples. The morphological point of some importance is the adoption of *o* as the masculine termination in nouns of an *a* base, instead of the *â* used in Marâthî. This appears to be originally a Prâkṛit termination, preserved in Koṅkaṇî, as in some other languages of the Neo-Sanskrit group. Thus the words *nara* in Sanskrit 'man' becomes *naro* in Prâkṛit, as *gṛiha* 'house' becomes *gharo*, and *karman* 'business' *kammo*. In working out such problems as these, there is no need therefore to have recourse to the Drâviḍian system of sounds in order to explain the change, under the supposition that it displays the action of a Drâviḍian language on the phonetics of an Âryan one, when the Prâkṛits explain it just as well. I will not stop to consider here whether the Prâkṛits themselves, or the Âryan populations in earlier times adopted this sound from the Drâviḍians, as it is a question beyond the scope of this paper to discuss. It may, however, be remarked that Koṅkaṇî is manifestly in the main formed on the basis of the Sanskṛit, which is destitute of short *o*; while Drâviḍian languages possess and largely employ this sound, having even different characters for the purpose of distinguishing it from the corresponding long vowel. But this is a phonetic change which admits of being explained through an Âryan system of sounds. Now these masculine nouns of the *a* base have a final *o* not only in Koṅkaṇî but also in Gujarâtî, just as Marâṭhî shares its general characteristic of a final *â* with Hindî. The philological laws, which rule these sounds, their origin, analogies and contrasts, may, perhaps, be discussed hereafter, when treating of the grammar of the language. In the meantime, it seems clear that Koṅkaṇî and Marâṭhî take their rise or descend from two different intermediate or Prâkṛit stages. The former has adopted the termination in *o*, which in S'aurasenî is *ao* and Apabhramsa *au*, in common with north-western Gauḍian tongues; while the latter has adopted *â*, which is in Mâgadhî *ac* and in Apabhramsa *ai* or *aa*, eventually contracted into *â*, in common with the south-eastern Gauḍian tongues. And thus the Sanskṛit *ghotakaḥ* 'horse,' after passing through a Prâkṛit stage, has at last become *ghoḍâ* in Marâṭhî, and *ghoḍo* in Koṅkaṇî.

This change is not confined to words derived from Sanskṛit alone, but is even extended to those borrowed from other languages: thus, for example, the Persian word for 'anchor' لنگر *(langar)*, which in Marâṭhî is *nângar*, becomes in Koṅkaṇî *nangor*. So far it is only the final *a* that is changed in Koṅkaṇî into *o*, but the medial *a* is also as often altered to the same sound. Thus the Sanskṛit word *varkara* 'goat,' which in Marâthî is changed into *bokaḍa*, becomes *bokoḍo* in Koṅkaṇî. Also the plural of feminine nouns in *î* is formed by adding *o*, thus *nadî* 'river' is formed into *nadîo* 'rivers', *boḍî* 'stick' into *boḍîo*, &c., which is one of the peculiarities of the Koṅkaṇî tongue; whereas in Marâṭhî such names assume â in the plural, e. g.:— '*bî*' a seed, '*byâ* or *biyâ*' seeds, '*gâḍî*' a carriage, '*gâḍyâ*,' and so on.

Again, the dative suffix in Marâṭhî is *lâ* or *sa*, while in Koṅkaṇî it is *ku*, which has been supposed to be identical with the Kânarese *ke*. But it is improbable that the present structure of the modern idiom of the Âryan stock is in any great degree indebted to non-Âryan influences; and Koṅkaṇî, in spite of its close proximity tc Draviḍian tongues, appears to owe little to the latter. The Koṅkaṇî *ku* has as much connexion with the Kânarese *ke*, as the Hindî *ko* has with the Tamil *ku*; for, it is now known that the Hindî sign of the dative is a regular form deduced from Sanskṛit, and common to some of the cognate languages of the same group. The Koṅkaṇî suffix *ku*, then, not only indicates that it possesses a distinct Âryan form, but supports also its claim to be considered as independent from Marâṭhî.[1]

Then the pronunciation of vowel sounds by the Koṅkaṇî Brâhmaṇs is broad, more like that of the Bengâlîs than of the Marâṭhâs. And, while in Marâṭhî the third person singular of verbs in the present tense ends in *o* and *e*, in Koṅkaṇî it does instead in *â*, and in the past in place of the Marâṭhî termination in *â* it ends in *o*, e. g.:— *vetâ* 'he goes,' *gelo* 'he went.'

It is time now to offer a few brief remarks on the origin of the word Koṅkaṇ and on that of the Koṅkaṇî language. Koṅkaṇ is derived by some from two Sanskṛit words कुः *(kuḥ)* 'earth' and कोणः *Koṇaḥ* 'corner,' i. e. 'corner of the earth,' and by others from Koḷkaṇ, or 'land of the Kolîs,' an aboriginal tribe of Western India, which word by a phonetic and graphic interchange of letters becomes

---

[1] See Mr. Brandreth's paper on the "*Gaurian compared with the Romance languages*" in the J. R. A. S. vol. XII. N. S. 1880, p. 343.

at last Koṅkaṇ. This change is further said to draw support from the fact of the lands of the Kols or Kolîs in Chota-Nâgpur being called Koḷkaṇ.[1] Again, that mythological personage Renuka, better known as Jamadagni's wife, or Paraśurâma's mother, is often styled in the Purâṇas *Konkaṇâ,* one of her son's numerous epithets being *Konkanâ-suta* or 'Koṅkaṇâ's son, whose name is so intimately associated with the legendary tales of the Koṅkaṇ. It is, however, far from easy to settle whether it was the name of the mother of Paraśurâma, which gave that designation to the country, or vice versâ. The latter seems probable from the circumstance of a supposed disciple of Agastya being called *Koṅkaṇar,* the adoption of this name being meant to identify him with the Koṅkaṇa country. The word Koṅkaṇ in a more or less modified form is also found in the writings of the mediæval writers, Muhammadan and others.

Now with regard to the origin of the Koṅkaṇî language, it seems that it is one of the Gauḍian languages of the north-western group, imported into the Koṅkaṇ by a colony of Brâhmaṇs from the north. And notwithstanding the lapse of centuries it is admitted that it still bears the stamp of Brâhmaṇical influence. To know from whence the colony came out, one must consult, in the absence of legitimate history, those legends and traditions, which are embodied in the *Sahyâdṛi Khaṇḍa* of the *Skaṇḍa Purâṇa,* considered to be a repository of every historical fact affecting the inhabitants of the Sahyâdṛi range of mountains and the low plains of the Koṅkaṇ. A complete MS. of this work is now extremely rare owing, as Grant Duff informs us, to the Peshwâs carefully suppressing or destroying its copies. The work is said to have been originally written by the *Madhyâdeshgâs,* or Brâhmaṇs dwelling in the middle country, which extends from Nâsik to Belgaum, and have probably in process of time emigrated to the Koṅkaṇ. But it must have also received during the course of centuries many interpolations of a more or less contradictory nature, and often from obscure and ignorant writers. Still, there are some fragments extant, which I once undertook to collect, animated by the feeling expressed in the old proverb *omne ignotum pro magnifico.* The edition of these fragments which I published in 1877, and the translation of which I have now completed, show the work to contain more mythology than history, more fiction than truth, and this embodied in a Sanskṛit which has but little regard for orthography and grammar. Difficult as it is to disentangle the thread of truth from the confused web of fiction, or of those hopeless mazes of legends and myths which everywhere abound, there are still incorporated into the work some local traditions of more or less worth, treasured up for centuries by the Brâhmaṇs of the Koṅkaṇ, who consider it to be their paladium. It may in consequence be utilized by patient and critical labour, obtaining some obscure hints, defective in chronological data though they be, from which grains of historical truth may be extracted. A hint of this kind is contained in the following distich :

त्रिहोत्रवासिनश्चैव पंचगौडांतरास्तथा ।
गोमाञ्चले स्थापितास्ते पंचक्रोश्यां कुशस्थल्यां ॥ ४८ ॥[2]

---

[1] J. R. A. Soc. vol. XVII. p. 370. [2] *Sahyâdri Khaṇḍa,* Bombay 1877, p. 305.

'Dwelling in Tṛihotṛa, and belonging to the Pañcha Gauḍa, they settled themselves at Gomâñchala and five *kós* of Kuśasthalî.'

Now Tṛihotṛa is evidently Tirhut, a district in the Bengal Presidency (lat. 25° 26′—26° 42′; long. 84° 58′—87° 11′).[1] It is said to receive this name from being bounded by three rivers, the Ganges, the Gunduck, and the Kosy. Gomâñchala is Goa, or the mountain of Goa, and Kuśasthalî is identified with the village opposite to the site of old Goa, now changed by the Portuguese into Cortalim. In the same work we are told, moreover, that it was Paraśuráma who brought these Brâhmaṇs from Tirhut, that they belonged to one of the five sub-divisions of the Gauḍa, which are Tṛihotṛas, Agnavaishas, Kanyâkubjas, Kanojas, and Maitrâyaṇas, and that they were originally of ten families or *gotras*, their names being Bhâradvâja, Kauśika, Vatsa, Kaundinya, Kaśyapa, Vasishṭha, Jamadagni, Viśvâmitra, Gautama, and Atrî; and lastly that the object Paraśurâma had in view in bringing them over to the Koṅkaṇ was to perform various sacrifices, especially *śrâddha*, or the religious rite of offering cakes and water to the spirits of progenitors. They were established, besides Goa and Kuśasthalî, at Maṭhagrâma (Margão), Kardalî (Curtorim), and other places with the family gods they brought with them from Tirhut. These gods were Mângirîś, Mahâdeva, Mahâlakśmî, Mhâlasâ, S'ântâ-Durgâ, Gâneśâ, Saptakoṭiśvara, and a host of others, brought here by their devotees. They were all commanded by Bhârgava or Paraśurâma to be located on "the mountain called Gomañta;" whence it appears that Gomâñchala or Gomâñta cannot be restricted to the narrow area of the island of Goa, but is to be applied to several other villages in the province of Sâlsette and elsewhere, where these gods are known to have been settled from time immemorial, such as Dîpavatî (Divar) where 'the seven sages' established the *liṅga* of Saptakoṭiśvara, now at Narvem, Hari-chûḍâmaṇî (Chorão), where there was a *tîrtha* 'or sacred pool,' as well as in Vareṇya (Verna).[2]

It results from the above that the Koṅkaṇ, especially Gomâñta, or Goa territory, was colonized by Paraśurâma with ten families of Brâhmaṇs from Tṛihotṛapura, or 'the city Tirhut,' and that they belong to one of the five sub-divisions of the Gauḍa-Brâhmaṇs. Now, although the Brâhmaṇs themselves divide their great class into simple and two-fold sections, or Gauḍa and Drâviḍa, or Northern and Southern Âryas of their sacerdotal community, the former of which is again sub-divided into five tribes, viz., Sarasvatî, Kanojî, Gauḍa or Gaur (Bengâlî), Maithila or Tirhutî, and Orissa or Oriya, still there are so many castes within castes, the Tirhutîs, for instance,

---

[1] Tirhut is elsewhere called *Tîrabhukti* 'bank-boundary.' Modern Tirhut is said to be the ancient kingdom of Videha. In this kingdom was born Sita, Râma's wife, and the daughter of Janaka, who was king of this country. Its first capital was Mithilâ, and the second Benares. The S'eṇvis have a special devotion of the holy city of Benares, which is also called Kâs'ı.

[2] Among the various *Mâhâtmyas*, describing the greatness of these *tîrthas* or places of pilgrimage, generally near rivers, Vareṇya is called Varuṇapura, a city of Varuna, Indian Neptune, the other places being *S'ankavâli* (Sancoale), *Agas'i*, or *Agânas'ini* (Agaçaim), &c.

being again, as noted above, broken up into five other sub-castes, that the subject is not only too vast to enter upon here, but foreign to the point under discussion. It is necessary, however, to remark that all spoken languages of the Indo-Âryan family are referred to these classes or sections of Gauḍas and Drâviḍas, the central seat of the former being Kanoj, the capital of the Kanyâkubjas, from which point its cognate tongues spread both east and west, stretching far to the south in the vicinity of Mangalore.

Again, the Gauḍa Brâhmaṇs from Tirhut, which is elsewhere called *Tîrabhukti,* who populated the Koṅkaṇ, though belonging to ten *gotras,* or corporate bodies, deriving their descent from ten *munis* or sages, were divided into ninety-six families. Each of these families is said to have settled itself in one village in Goa, giving thereby rise to the denomination, in accordance with the number of villages, of the two provinces of Goa, viz., Tisuary and Sâlsette. The former means thirty villages from *tîs* 'thirty,' and *vâḍî* 'villages,' while the latter means sixty-six, from *shaṭ* and *shashṭi,* making up together ninety-six, or *śaṇṇav* in Sanskṛit, the origin of the class name—Senoy, Sinay, S'aṇavî, or S'eṇvî, by which these Brâhmaṇs are known to the present.[1] Speaking of the sixty-six families of Sâlsette we are told, in the said *Sahyâdri Khaṇḍa,*[2] that three of the ten *gotras,* viz., Kautsa or Kauśika, Vatsa, and Kauṇḍinya, which were again sub-divided into ten families, were settled at Kuśasthaḷî (Cortalim), and Kardalî (Curtorim), and that they were much respected by kings, were handsome, well-behaved, and skilful. Then other families are said to have been distributed amongst the villages of Sâlsette, viz., *Loṭlî* (Loutolim), *Vareṇya* (Verna), Maṭhagrâma (Margão), and others; amongst those of the Ilhas or Tisvaḍî, *Chûḍâmaṇî* (Chorão), which is called *mahâkshetra* or 'great country or place,' Dîpavatî (Divar), and, lastly, we are informed that in the *Dvâdaśapura* were established twelve families, and that in course of time they very naturally multiplied themselves. The word *Dvâdaśapura* may probably be an ancient name of Bardez, or *bârâ-deś* 'twelve countries,' which *Dvâdaśapura* also means, *dvâdaśa* in Sanskṛit being equivalent to the Marâṭhî *bârâ* 'twelve.' Then we are told that in the centre of Gomâṅchala was established the caste of Kirvanta Brâhmaṇs, and in the centre of Pañchacrośa, which may be an area of five *kos* (about ten miles), or perhaps modern Pañchmahal, twelve other Brâhmaṇs.

Now, with regard to the time or epoch when this colonization of the Koṅkaṇ by Paraśurâma with the Tirhutî Brâhmaṇs took place, it is a problem of difficult solution. The complete absence of a single

---

[1] It is strange how fanciful and far-fetched the etymologies given by some writers are. Of S'envî, for example, Dr. Wilson writes : "This name is probably a nick-name. Some will have it that it originates in a sectarian fable that the Shénavis are the offspring of a Brâhman and a girl who was found by him gathering *Shén* or cow-dung, whom he made a mother. Perhaps the word is a corruption of the Kânarese *shánbhog* 'a village-accountant.' *Indian Caste,* Bombay 1877, vol. II. p. 29.

With regard to the word Sâlsette Mr. F. N. Xavier says :—"*Sasty,* alias *Sat-poty* (37 livros ou contas correntes, em allusão a outras tantas corporações). *Bosq. Hist.* das Communidades. New Goa, 1852, Pt. II. p. 6.

[2] *Op. Cit.* p. 311 et seq.

date in the Purâṇas compels us to have recourse to circumstantial evidence only. The mythic fight of Paraśurâma, and his subsequent populating with those tribes of Brâhmaṇs his *kshetra,* may be taken for what it is worth ; but the persistence with which the tradition of his having reclaimed this narrow strip of the land from the sea recurs in one shape or another along the whole western coast of India, may possibly shadow forth a geological fact, the gradual elevation of the sea-board.

The Paraśurâman era is fixed by some Vedantists at 600 B.C., but this date seems too early for the colonization of the Koṅkaṇ with the Brâhmaṇs. Then, again, the family-gods which this colony brought with them to the Koṅkaṇ, and especially to Goa, their principal place, are mostly those worshipped by the S'aiva sect, which does not appear to have arisen before the seventh century of our era, this being also the time when the decay of Buddhism brought about great linguistic changes, and laid the foundation of modern idioms, the western members of the Âryan group taking precedence of the eastern ones, as Eastern India is said to have then been rather sparsely peopled by the Âryas.

These Brâhmaṇs might have been introduced into the Koṅkaṇ by some zealous prince, expecting them to propagate Brâhmaṇism in the way Âdiśura or Âdîśvara, king of Bengâl, did. Finding that religion was at a low ebb, he is said to have sent to the Râjâ of Kanoj or Kanyâkubja for some high-caste Brâhmaṇs, in the eleventh century, to revive it, and then raised their descendants, forbidding intermarriage between these Brâhmaṇs and the families which had previously settled in Bengâl, until no less than one hundred and fifty families sprang from them. The Tirhutî Brâhmaṇs, moreover, might have become divided in the Koṅkaṇ into ninety-six tribes or families, earning thereby the patronymic of S'eṇvîs or S'aṇavîs. They are also called Sârasvata Brâhmaṇs, this designation being derived from their early settlement near the river Sarasvatî in Northern India. They settled in different villages in the Koṅkaṇ, just as the one hundred and fifty families, brought into Bengâl by king Âdiśûra, are said to have settled, a hundred in Vâvendra, and fifty in Râḍha. Some of these tribes are even now regarded as Kulîna or 'noble,' in which respect they resemble also the S'aṇavîs, who are considered more aristocratic than others, according to their descent from some of the ten Munis, who first colonised Goa. Then, again, just as the Kanouj Brâhmaṇs brought with them some Kâyasthas or 'writers,' from whom sprang other various tribes, the Tirhutî Brâhmaṇs might have as well brought with them to the Koṅkaṇ other castes, such as artizans of the Vaiśya caste, which have in course of time multiplied, and now form the numerous castes and sub-castes of Chardós, S'ûdras, and others, including those of artizans named *Kânsârs,* or 'braziers,' *Sonârs* or 'goldsmiths,' &c., which are generally absorbed in that of *Chardós,* and which, besides the Brâhmaṇs and the aboriginal races, constitute the motley population of Goa.

In the absence of trustworthy evidence, and of chronological data, enshrouded as the beginning of their colony is in a mystery, it is a mere matter of conjecture to say that these Brâhmaṇs were called by the Kadamba kings of Goa, when the latter were independent, and not feudatories of the Châlukyas. They may as well have been called by the latter, or by the Chôḷas, Raṭṭas, Yâdavas, or any other race or dynasty, all of whom might have held sway over this part of the Koṅkaṇ severally and at diverse periods for centuries before the arrival of the Portuguese. All depends upon the exact date of their advent here from Northern India, which cannot at present be ascertained, and upon the sectarian leanings of the sovereign, under whose patronage they first settled in the Koṅkaṇ. That prince must have himself been a member of the S'aiva sect, or at least favourable to them, since almost all the S'aṇavî Brâhmaṇs belong to it, and the temples, which were destroyed by the Portuguese missionaries in the province of Sâlsette about the year 1560, and a list of which has been fortunately preserved, building on their ruins Christian churches, were dedicated to Mahâdeva, to the Devî, and other personages, holding a conspicuous place in the pantheon of this sect.[1]

To throw as much light as possible into this obscure subject of South Indian chronology, I may, perhaps, be allowed to enter into a few details regarding the dynasties, and their religious faiths, holding sway for some centuries over this part of India. The first in the list, hitherto known, is the dynasty of the Kadambas, and next that of the Châlukyas, a powerful tribe of Râjputs, who are said to have come from Oudh (Pañchâla) in the neighbourhood of the intensively Brâhmaṇical kingdom of Kanyâkubja or Kanoj, which always took part with the Brâhmaṇs against the Buddhists. These Châlukyas were established at Kaliâṇapura near Beder in the western part of the Nizâm's territory, in 250 A. D. Their power reached its acme during the fourth and fifth centuries, and became extinct in 1182, when the Yâdavas conquered their kingdom.

Some centuries before, the Goa territory appears to have fallen under the rule of the Kadambas of Banavâsi, which still exists where it stood in the time of Ptolemy, about 60 miles westwards from Harihara;[2] but whether it was the latter dynasty, or that of the Châlukyas who invited the Brâhmaṇs of Tirhut to settle in the Koṅkaṇ, it is impossible to tell. The rulers of both of these families appear to have been devoted to Brâhmaṇism, especially the Châlukyas, who were, moreover, neighbours formerly of an intensely Brâhmaṇical kingdom. Eventually, this part of the Koṅkaṇ passed under the sway of the Râyas of Vijayanâgara, whose king Bukka is favourably known as the patron of Sâyaṇâchârya, the commentator of the Ṛigveda. From the house of the Râyas of Vijayanâgara, it was conquered by the Muhammadan dynasty known as Bahmanî, which held sway for 150 years, from 1347 A. D., over a great part of the Dakhaṇ and Koṅkaṇ, until it was divided into five smaller kingdoms, Goa falling to the share of the kingdom of Bijâpur, founded by Adil Shâh or Khan, or Idalcão, as the Portuguese chroniclers call him, in 1489 A. D. It is unnecessary to repeat here how from this last ruler Goa was conquered for the Portuguese by Affonso d'Albuquerque in 1510 A. D.

---

1 Bosq. Hist. das Communidades, *ut supra*, Pt. II. p. 138-139.

2 The Legends of the shrine of Harihara, by Revd. T. Foulkes, Madras 1876, p. 10.

But to go a little further back than the time of the Âryan colonization of the Koṅkaṇ.

A tradition current in the country, ascribes the early colonization of this part of the Koṅkaṇ to a rude people, who came up from the southern region of Kânaḍa, and, finding it unoccupied and with a fertile soil, began to cultivate it. This is said to have taken place at a time immemorial, of which there is no record in documentary history. In course of time agriculture improved, the country grew rich, and trade became developed, which attracted the notice of a powerful prince, who descended from the Ghâṭs and conquered this rude but peaceful population, and then introduced high-class Hindûs, dividing amongst them as well as amongst the aboriginal colonizers of the country the land, which was distributed into villages, each village paying a fixed tax to the royal treasury. We are not told who this prince was, nor when the high-class Hindûs were imported there; but a traditional embodiment of these most probably historical facts, is found in early Portuguese chroniclers, who, far from contemning mere traditions, collected them with no little concern and advantage, well aware that to deprive man of tradition amounts to removing from him a useful instrument of knowledge. The Portuguese historians, who have utilised these traditions, are João de Barros in his Decada II. Liv. 5, Cap. 1; Diogo do Couto, Decada IV. Liv. 10; Padre Francisco de Souza in his *Oriente Conquistado*, vol. I. Conq. I. Dec. 2, para. 56; Braz d'Albuquerque in his *Commentarios*, and several others.

As regards the name of the prince above alluded to, no document is available, except perhaps the discovery of a few copper-plates in the old city of Goa relating to the Kadamba dynasty. These *tâmrapaṭṭas*, which according to some are said to have consisted of three, and according to others of two plates, were found underground in 1641, and were sent to Lisbon on 23rd January 1727. A copy of their translation into Portuguese was, however, preserved, and is published in the *Gabinete Litterario*, vol. I. pp. 16 *et seq.*, and elsewhere. It results from the contents of these metallic records that in 1090 [1] A. D., Jayakeśî II., who was a contemporary of the Châlukya Emperor Vikramâditya, whose reign continued from 1076 to 1127 A. D., was a ruler of Goa. We are told elsewhere [2] that the Koṅkaṇ rose against him, but the rebellion was quelled by his general Sindavanśa. And it was probably subsequent to this occurrence that the tables were inscribed, containing provisions for a commercial treaty with the neighbouring ports.

An inference drawn by the writers who have studied the subject is, that three centuries before Jayakeśi II. held sway in Goa, the Brâhmaṇic colony must have been brought down to the Koṅkaṇ by some hitherto unknown prince. Jayakeśi II. ruled at Goa in 1090, being preceded by nine other princes of his house, over a space of two centuries, and allowing the least a hundred years, not for the aboriginal colonizers from Kânaḍa to bring the land under cultivation

---

[1] The *Gabinete* has 1054; but a more correct MS. copy gives the above date.
[2] J. B. B. R. As. Soc. vol. XI. p. 234-44.

to the extent of rendering it worthy of the ambition of a prince, but to raise it to the state of civilization in which the first Kadamba conqueror found it, it must have been about 790 A. D. that that unknown prince invited the Brâhmaṇs to settle in the Koṅkaṇ, that is 1090 years ago from the present time. It may have been earlier than this, but there is nothing in the nature of things to controvert this statement; and the village communities, which form a notable feature in the policy of that government, might have well been introduced there in that century, as is alleged by a writer [1] who had made this subject his speciality, although he allows the long period of two hundred years to four rulers, instead of to nine, as mentioned above, which is a figure correctly given in a trustworthy manuscript document. This date tallies, moreover, with that religious revival, which about that time gave a new impetus to Âryan colonization. The tributary regulations agreed upon between the Hindû sovereign of the Koṅkaṇ and the village communities were carried on during the reign of the Muhammadan rulers, and when the Portuguese conquered the country, King John III., by his decree dated the 26th February 1526, maintained the same system, which was, moreover, confirmed by that of King Peter II. on the 6th March 1682.

But this is a digression. To return to the Koṅkaṇî Brâhmaṇs, there are, it is true, several Vaishṇava families among these Brâhmaṇs, but they seem, besides being in minority, to have risen at a later date, about the latter part of the twelfth century, the epoch of the reformer Râmânuja; while the S'aivas claim an antiquity, which if not prior to, is at least coeval with, S'aṅkarâchârya, whose epoch is not yet fixed, but generally admitted to be at least five centuries before that of the Vaishṇava reformer. There being no census taken in Portuguese India, based on the difference of sects, it is not possible at present to state the exact proportion the number of the Vaishṇavas bears to that of the S'aivas, but the latter are said without contradiction to preponderate over the former.

These Tṛihotras, or S'aṇavîs, are in one place in the *Sûta-sanhita*, described as "Brâhmaṇs deeply read in the Vedas and Vedangas, devoted to the six *karmas*, having subdued their passion by means of *mantras*, herbs, penances, and *yoga*" (ch. 16. sk. 4-5). In another place of the *Sahyâdṛi Khaṇḍa* they are said to be, along with the Kanoujâs, "eaters of flesh and devourers of fish." (*Uttara Khaṇḍa* or Pt. II. of my edition, before referred to, ch. I. sk. 11, p. 302). On account of their eating fish, which, however, they are said to call, as if to extenuate the gravity of the sin, *jalashâka* or 'water-vegetable;' other Brâhmaṇs look down upon the S'aṇavîs and deny them the six works or rights of Brâhmaṇism. The Koṇkaṅasth or Chitpâvan Brâhmaṇs, for instance, call them *Trikarmî* (*i. e.* men of three privileges or functions, viz., *adhyayan* 'study of the S'âstras,' *dân*, 'alms-giving,' and *yâjan* 'sacrificing by deputy, while professing themselves to be *shaṭkarmî* or men of six privileges, viz., *adhyâpan*, 'teaching of the S'âstras,' *pratigraha*, 'accepting gifts,' *yâjan*,

---

[1] F. N. Xavier in the Bosq. Hist. das Communidades, Goa 1852, Pt. II. p. 6.

'sacrificing personally,' and the abovementioned three rights conceded to the S'aṇavîs. But from a perusal of their arguments it appears that the latter are also *shaṭkarmîs,* although it is not incumbent on them to practise all these works, to perform all these functions. Their adversaries found their opposition on a legend in the *shatpraśna kalpa Latica,* wherein it is stated that the Gauḍa Brâhmaṇs, during a famine raging for twelve years, ate fish, and lost therefore three out of their six rights; whereas the Northern Brâhmaṇs of the Gauḍa division eat not only fish, but also flesh meat, and are yet in possession of six rights.[1]

The S'aṇavîs have amongst them some who are *vatandârs* or hereditary officers, and officiating priests or *pûjârîs* in their temples; but most of them have now become entirely secularised, and show a pronounced tendency towards Western culture. Some of them are, as above remarked, Vaishṇavas, and others *Smârtas* 'observers of the *Smṛitis* or the books of law,' or S'aivas. They have their own *gurus, âchâryas* or *svâmis* of their caste, living in their own *maṭhs* or hermitages at Goa, Nâsik, Benares, and elsewhere, and are not subject to the jurisdiction of the ecclesiastical authority of either the S'aṅkarâchârya or the Mâdhavâchârya of the Drâviḍian Brâhmaṇs. Since the arrival of the Portuguese, and the over-zeal of their missionaries in converting them, various factions have broken out from time to time amongst them, known under the name of Narvenkar, Bârdeshkar, Peḍnekar, Kuḍâldeshkar, Kuśasṭhalî, Khadapé, Bhâlâvalkar, Loṭlikar, Divâḍkar, and so on, each having its different *taṭa,* while those, who stand aloof from the factions thus named from the districts to which they originally belonged, are called *kevaḷa-śaṇavîs* or 'pure S'aṇavîs.'

These were the Brâhmaṇs, or their ancestors, who introduced into the Koṅkaṇ a new language, now known as Koṅkaṇî, along with the S'aîva form of Brâhmaṇism, most probably, and that admirable organization of village communities, which has given rise to a voluminous and interesting literature in Portuguese language, scarcely known beyond the boundaries of Goa. The institution and administration of these *communidades* or *gancarias,* or 'assemblage of villagers,' a Portuguese adaptation from the Koṅkaṇî *gâum,* Sk. *grâma* 'village' and *gâumkâr* 'villager,' are certainly worthy of an attentive study through all its stages, both before and after the Portuguese conquest of Goa.

Having referred to the tradition concerning the descent of the Koṅkaṇî S'aṇavîs or S'eṇvîs from the Tṛihotṛas or Maithila Brâhmaṇs of the Gauḍa division, it would certainly add some support to this statement, if one could trace genealogically the Koṅkaṇî language from the Maithilî, a dialect spoken in the district of Tirhut, about Muzafarpûr and Darbhanga, and called after the ancient city of Mithilâ, the capital of Videha, or modern Tirhut. But there is an absolute want of materials at present to enable us to institute such an interesting comparison, except a few extracts from one

---

[1] सारस्वत ब्राह्मण &c. Bom. 1870.

kîrtan by the poet Vidyâpati, the language of which is said to closely resemble that spoken at the present time in Tirhut. This dialect exhibits, according to Dr. Hoernle,[1] unmistakeable similarities to the neighbouring Bengâlî and Nepâlî, the latter being closely allied to Western Gauḍian languages in both its morphological and syntactical relations. Mr. Beames tells us that the preterites गेल and केल and such like, now obsolete in Bengâl proper, are still in use in Tirhut; these bear close resemblance to the Koṅkaṇî *gelo, kelo,* &c. Again, the past tense in Maithilî *delchhe* 'he has given' is in Eastern Hindî *dihale vaṭe,* while in Koṅkaṇî it is *dilo, dili,* or *dilem,* according to one of the three genders of the subjects of the verb, and in Marâṭhî *dela áhe* with the corresponding genders.

Some other analogies in manners, customs, and sectarian particularities, existing between the Bengâlî and Koṅkaṇî Brâhmaṇs, may perhaps be adduced here in support of the theory of their common origin. The S'aṇavîs, like the Bengâlîs, freely rub their heads with the cocoanut oil. They are both fond of rice gruel or *pej*, and of fish. They are in Koṅkaṇ addressed with the honorific prefix of *Bâb*, which in Bengâl becomes *Băbu.* Their great god Mângiris' (Mânges') has temples raised or dedicated to him both in Goa and in Tirhut.

The Maithila Brâhmaṇs are said to use a variety of Devanâgarî characters in their writings, and that even works in Sanskṛit are written in this Tirhutîya character.[2] It would be interesting to learn the affinity between these letters and those originally employed by the S'aṇavîs or S'eṇvîs in the Koṅkaṇ. Were ancient MS. of the latter available, with the archaic form of their speech, when first introduced into this side of India, the ethnological relations of the two classes of Brâhmaṇs might have more easily been fixed by the examination of their languages, thus affording an historical support to a traditional statement. The modern Koṅkaṇî, however, is utterly insufficient for such a purpose, its language-boundaries being far from well-marked.

Although the basis of the language is Sanskṛit, Koṅkaṇî has received at irregularly succeeding periods accretions of foreign words, rendering it in this respect a precise counterpart of several modern European languages, and indicating in its process of development the successive stages of progress or evolution it has passed through before arriving at the present state.

To give an illustration of the constituent elements of the Koṅkaṇî, one must begin with its basis, which is, as above said, entirely Sanskṛit, all the rest being successive developmental formations. The words, derived from Sanskṛit, may be divided, following the familiar native verbal divisions, adopted by Oriental philologists, into *Tatsamas* or words used in the same form as in Sanskṛit except in pronunciation, such as the rejection of the final

---

[1] Calcutta Review, vol. LXVI., 1878, p. 758. Cf. Comp. Gram. of Modern Âryan Lang. vol. I. p. 85.
[2] Dr. Wilson's *Indian Caste*, vol. II. p. 193.

syllable ; *Tadbhâvas* or words originally derived from Sanskṛit, but altered in the process of Prâkṛitic transformation, without obscuring their etymology ; and lastly *Deśajas,* or words borrowed from the non-Âryan aborigines, or invented by Âryan immigrants, in post-Sanskṛitic times.

A parallel system of divisions of words exists amongst most of the modern European languages. The latin word *cancer* is in Portuguese *cancro,* which is a *Tatsama* ; while the Portuguese *bater* (to beat), not being derived directly from the Latin *verberare,* but from the vulgar *batuere,* the latter being the corresponding Prâkṛit form, so to speak, of the Romance languages, becomes a *Tadbhâva,* and *bacalhaú* 'cod-fish', an aboriginal word, a *Deśaja.* I have chosen the word *bacalhaú* to illustrate the Romance *deśajas,* although not unaware of its difficulties. Notwithstanding philologers wrangling about it, it is derived neither from the Latin *baculum* (the stick,) with which the dried fish is kept exposed, as the name is applied to both the fresh and dried cod-fish, nor from the German *block,* which is a generic name for fish. It is indeed a Mediterranean *deśaja* word. These three groups of words are then such as are little altered from the original, and hence called *Tatsama, i.e.,* 'the same as it ;' or such as are changed in coming down, through ages, to us, in the mouths of the people, all changes being however subject to certain phonetic rules which would be out of our scope to discuss here, and called *Tadbhâva, i e.,* of the nature of it (Sanskṛit) ; and lastly new adoptions from the aborigines or country people, whence called *deśajas,* which literally signifies 'indigenous' or 'country-born.'

Here follow a few words, out of a large number, in Koṅkaṇî which are *Tatsamas,* giving in the opposite column their Sanskṛit originals :—

Koṅkaṇî.	Sanskrit.
Vâṭ, 'road'	वाट (vâṭa).
Mârg, 'road'	मार्ग (mârga).[1]
Dharṇî, 'earth'	धरणि (dharaṇi).
Nâgar, 'city'	नागर (nâgara).
Angan, 'court-yard'	अङ्गन (aṅgana).
Sopon, 'seat'	सोपान (sopâna).
Nisaṇ, 'ladder'	निसणी (nisaṇî).
Sarṇ, 'broom'	सरणी (saraṇî).
Sâr, 'pulp'	सार (sâra).
Dant, 'tooth'	दन्त (danta).

---

[1] In Koṅkaṇî there are several words, which are both *Tatsamas* and *Tadbhâvas,* or which have been transmitted to it directly from Sanskṛit and through Prâkṛit, but having different meanings ; thus the word *mârg,* descended from Sanskṛit *mârga,* is applied to a road ; while the Prâkṛit *maggo* is applied to the parting of the hair.

Konkaṇî.	Sanskṛit.
Komól, 'lotus-flower'	कमल (kamala).
Kambôl 'blanket'	कम्बल (kambala).
Kîḍó, 'worm'	कीट (kîṭa).
Râzâ, 'king'	राजा (râjâ).

To the above examples several more may be added, the identity of which could be easily verified, as direct descendants from Sanskṛit; but those given here are sufficient for our purpose.

The following words are Tadbhâvas, which are again sub-divided into *early Tadbhâvas*, or words come down through the Prâkṛit, and *late Tadbhâvas*, or words inported into the language in post-Buddhistic times. Some of the early *Tadbhâvas* have been so altered in their developmental process as to lose all resemblance to Sanskṛit; while the late ones have not yet had time to become thus changed. In the following list, next to the Koṅkaṇî word, is given its corresponding Prâkṛit, from which it is derived, and then the original Sanskṛit.

Konkaṇî.	Prâkṛit.	Sanskṛit.
Deo, 'God'	देओ (deo)	देव (deva).
Bokoḍó, 'goat'	बक्करो (bakkaro)	वर्कर (varkara).
Vinchu, 'scorpion'	विञ्छुओ (vinchuo)	वृश्चिक (vriśchika).
Kumbâr, 'potter'	कुम्भारो (kumbhâro)	कुम्भकार (kumbhakâra).
Soṇâr, 'goldsmith'	सोणारो (soṇâro)	सुवर्णकार suvarṇakâra.
Nâll, 'cocoa-nut'	णारियलो (ṇârielo)	नारिकेल (nârikela).
Suî, 'needle'	सुई (sûî)	सूची (sûchî).
Bhâo, 'brother'	भाओ (bhâo)	भ्राता (bhrâtâ).
Ghâó, 'wound'	घाओ (ghâo)	घात (ghâta).
Uns, 'sugar-cane'	उच्छू (uchchhû)	इक्षु (ikśu).
Kam, 'work'	कम्म (kamma)	क्रम (krama).
Surî, 'knife'	छुरी (churî)	क्षुर (kśura).
S'et, 'field'	छेत्तं (chettam)	क्षेत्र (kśetra).
Masui, 'fish'	मच्छो (machchho)	मत्स्य (matsya).
Kanṭo, 'thorn'	कंटओ (kanṭao)	कण्टक (kaṇṭaka).
Matem, 'head'	मंथओ (manthao)	मस्तक (mastaka).
Naim, 'river'	णई (ṇaî)	नदी (nadî).

To this list innumerable such words may be added; but the circumscribed limits of this paper forbid more additions. We hasten therefore to treat of the other elements entering into the formation of Koṅkaṇî.

To begin then with the *Desajas*. On their arrival in the Konkan, the Tirhutian immigrants, coming in contact with the aborigines, whose modern representatives are Gauḍes, Karvîs, Kuṇbîs, and Farazes or Mahârs, could not help taking in many of their words in forming a language for mutual understanding. Their native idiom, the Sarasvatî Bâlabanî, or "the speech of the children of the banks of the Sarasvatî," as it is called by their descendants even now, was subjected to some modification, which eventually gave rise to another provincial tongue, the Konkaṇî. Now what language the aborigines of the Konkaṇ originally spoke, we have no means of ascertaining. It was probably a dialect of one of the Drâviḍian languages. Such words as *gundó* 'stone' (in Kânarese *gunḍu* means any thing round, such as a cannon-ball), *duru* 'money,' *tantim* 'egg', *komp* 'a cottage', *dol* 'a drum,' *morvol* 'washerman,'[1] and others can be directly traced to any of the known Drâviḍian tongues; while there are a few which have been adopted from them, although having a somewhat different meaning. Thus we have the word *mâṛ* or *mâḍ* which is also used in Marâṭhî. This word has from time immemorial been admitted into the Konkaṇî language from Drâviḍian sources; but, while in Tamil, in the shape of *maram*, and in Kânarese in that of *mara*, it simply means 'a tree', in Konkaṇî it is applied to the cocoanut tree alone, on account of this being perhaps the tree *par excellence*. And then with a prefix or a slight change in the termination, it is used for the technical purpose of a rude botanical classification, naming other varieties of palms, thus:—*birla-mâr* 'Caryota urens', *târ-mâr* 'Borassus flabeliformis,' *khajûr-mâr* 'Phœnix dactylifera,' *marî*, a diminutive form, (in Marâṭhî माडा *mâḍâ*) 'a young tree', to designate the more delicate palm, yielding the supâri-nut, and known under the scientific name of 'Areca Catechu,' and so on. A similar system of classification holds good in respect to the genus Ficus and it species, but the names are derived from Sanskṛit, *viz.*, वट (vaṭa), from which is derived *voḍ* for the Banyan tree in Konkaṇî, along with *rum-voḍ*, *voḍî*, and so on. The purely *Désaja* words used in Konkaṇî are numerous, and refer exclusively to objects formerly unknown to the northern immigrants, such as animals, plants, &c., although even for some of these they invented descriptive names with the aid of their mother-tongue only. They borrowed also words relating to agriculture of the kind formerly unknown to them. Here follows a list of some of these and other terms, which cannot be easily traced to any known source, whether Sanskṛit or Drâviḍian :—

Aḍo 'a fence,' *adsor* 'an unripe cocoanut,' *adoli* 'a cutting instrument,' *aloṇ* 'an irrigation basin,' *mero* 'a larger fence,' *beḷḷô* 'a heap of earth,' *churot* 'a palm-leaf,' *coḍó* 'a rice-magazine' or 'granary,' *konḍó* 'a cane-measure,' *murcunḍó* 'an agricultural instrument,' *sinḍi* 'an

---

[1] In other Neo-Âryan tongues the word for 'washerman' is धोबी (Dhobî), probably derived from Sanskrit root धाव् (*dhâv*) 'to wash' in vulgar language, whence the Konkanî *dhovum*, and Marâthî *dhune* 'to wash', and *dhupane* 'to be washed'; while in classical Sanskrit it is used in the sense of 'to run,' 'to flow.'

account-book,' *terḷo* 'a watchman,' *zabló* 'a coir-sac,' and a thousand others.

As in course of time the Koṅkaṇ became subjected to Kânarese rulers, and remained under their sway for some centuries, a good many words from their language must have been imported into Koṅkaṇî. For how long this rule was continued we have at present no means at our disposal to determine, but the historical documents hitherto known place the Koṅkaṇ, as early as the 10th century of our era, under the sway of the Kadambas of Banavâsi, or Jayantapura, and again in the 14th century under that of the Râyas of Vidyânâgara or Vijayanâgara, one of whom, by name Harihara, is said to have restored, with the aid of his prime minister Vidyâraṇya Mâdhava, the ancient S'aiva temple of S'rî Sapta-Koṭiśvara at Narvem, not far from the old city of Goa, which had been demolished, through their iconoclastic over-zeal, by Muhammadans under Mulik Tubliga in 1312 A.D.[1] At the courts of both of these rulers Kânarese was spoken. It is on this account, perhaps, that Koṅkaṇî is permeated with nouns and interjections which are evidently Kânarese; thus, *koṭâ* from Kânarese *akoṭâ*, expressive of sorrow; *agô*, 'lo! behold,' applied to women and girls of lower classes, while to those of higher classes is applied *are*, which in Marâṭhî is addressed to men; *shi* from Kânarese *chi* 'Fie!' denoting disgust, and so on. *Agô* is entirely different from *agé*, which is derived from Sanskrit आर्ये (*ârye*) through the Prâkrit अज्जे (*azze*), Marâṭhî अगे (*age*), in Koṅkaṇî variably addressed to old women, meaning originally respectable.

The kings of Kânaḍa were followed by the Muhammadan Sultâns of Bijâpur, under whose rule many Persian terms were introduced into Koṅkaṇî. These words refer principally to the revenue administration of the country, and are, in proportion to the other elements of the language, in considerable minority. As instances of the above are appended below the following terms:—

KOṄKAṆÎ.	PERSIAN.
Hak, (Portuguese *acca*) 'right'	حق (hakk).
Adaú, 'payment'	ادا (adá).
Faidó 'profit'	فايده (Fáida).
Môr, 'seal'	مهر (Muhr).
Sher, 'city'	شهر (shahr).
Ghoroz, 'wish'	غرض (gharaz).
Fursot, 'leisure'	فرصت (furśat).
Gun, 'mode'	گنهه (gúna).
Hozar, 'a thousand'	هزار (hazár).

[1] See my notes on S'rî Sapta-Koṭis'vara in the *Indian Antiquary*, Vol. III. p. 194-195.

Koṅkaṇî.	Persian.
Sissó, 'a vial or bottle'	شیشه (shisha).
Padsha, 'king'	پادشاه (pádsháh).
Doriâ, 'sea' (*zendicè zraia*)	دریا (darya.)
Dusman, 'enemy' (*zendicè dush-mainîu*)	دشمن (dushman).
Tâl, 'deceit'	ٹال (tál).
Koroch, 'expense'	خرج (kharj).
Chacor, 'servant'	چاکر (chákar).
Gulam, 'slave'	غلام (ghulám).

Lastly, a quite foreign element, one that has not hitherto influenced any other Indian language, was added to the Koṅkaṇî, when the Portuguese conquered Goa. From 1510 A.D. to the present, an enormous amount of Portuguese words have been introduced into the Koṅkaṇî speech, and although many of these Portuguese words have synonyms or equivalent expressions in the vernacular Koṅkaṇî, still the people have acquired the habit of mixing the Portuguese terms with Koṅkaṇî, in so unsystematic and capricious a manner as to cause the hearing of such a jumble to become extremely painful to cultivated or delicate ears. Here follow two specimens of this mongrel Koṅkaṇî in the shape of popular lyric poetry, called *manḍó*, originally the name of a country-dance, and of other songs, such as *zotîs*, sung by the lower classes amongst the native Christians of the Koṅkaṇ on the arrival of the *vod*, Sanskrit व्रात (vrâta), or marriage procession, beginning with the verse *ailó amchó vod*, 'our procession is arrived,' and so on, of which the pure Hindûs have never been guilty. The Portuguese words are italicised.

Vell zalló *bençavanchó*,
Bitor *abalo* zalâ *mâiamchó*,
Estilo xicounchac etai tucâ amchâ goracho,
Nourê bâî mure amche.[1]

Agi tucâ apoun anvem ariló,
Ulounchac muzó *sentimento*,
Cossoloch tucâ mugean dium nuzó *agradecimento*,
Senhor doutor amchea.[2]

Some of these poetical compositions have a beauty of their own, which cannot be done justice to when translated into another language; for a translation can only render in a very feeble manner the beauty and force of the original. The principal defect, however, of these popular songs in Koṅkaṇî is, that precision of language is wantonly sacrificed to the exigencies of the rhyme. No regard is paid to orthography in the above pieces, although grammatical rules are strictly observed, Portuguese words being treated as so many Koṅkaṇî ones, subject to the same inflectional forms. I append in a footnote below their translations, which may be easily passed over by the reader able to furnish a better rendering of them.[3]

---

[1] *Ramalhetinho de Cancões em Portuguez e Concani*, by M. V. d'Abreu, New-Goa 1866, p. 24. [2] *Ibid* 28.

[3] It is the time of benedictions,
Inside are concerned old relations,
Who come to teach you our home-style,
Our dear pretty little bride !

I have brought you to-day with a call,
To speak my deep affection,
No words can express my thanks at all,
Our beloved physician !

An attentive perusal of the above lines indicates plainly, how saturated Koṅkaṇî has become with Portuguese. It is not a mere importation of a few terms for new objects of Portuguese origin. These latter we find in some of the Western tongues, such as Marâṭhî and Gujarâtî. In Molesworth's Marâṭhî Dictionary, for instance, one meets with the following words:— मेज (*mez*) 'table,' from the Portuguese *meza,* (Kánarese ಮೇಜು *(meju)*, Gujarâtî મેજ *(mez)*; लवाद (*lavâd*) 'umpire' from *louvado* ; बरात (*barât*) 'a suit at cards,' from *barata* ; लिलाम (*lilám*) 'auction' from *leilão* ; कमीज (*camîz*) 'shirt' from *camiza* ; भुतावें (butâvem) 'button' from *butão* ; काजा (câza) 'button-hole' from *caza,* and several others. But these vocables were introduced into Marâṭhî, and have now been welded into it, forming part and parcel of that language, simply owing to the former intercourse and commerce between the natives of Mahârâshtra and of Gujarât and the Portuguese. They are the relics of the sway once held by the Lusitanian people over a great portion of the sea-board of Western India. Vocables introduced in this fashion, by means of such an intercourse, carried on by one great nation with other peoples or countries, are common enough in the English language, wherein we find the words *cherub, jubilee, manna,* and *sabbath* derived from Hebrew; *alcohol, caliph, firman,* and *talisman* from Arabic; *barbican, scimitar, sherbet,* and *tiffin* from Persian; *bangalow, jungle, palanquin* and *toddy* from Hindustânî; *bantam, cautchue,* and *gong,* from Malay; *nankin, tea,* and *hyson* from Chinese; and *bey, sash,* and *seraglio* from Turkish.

This is not, however, the case with Koṅkaṇî. Portuguese is mixed with that language by the right of domain over the Koṅkaṇ, just as words from Romans, Angles, Jutes, and Saxons, were introduced into English by their conquest of Britain, or from Arabs into Spanish and Portuguese. Thus *ceaster, coln, strot* in English are derived from the Latin *castra, colonia,* and *strata,* or *cow, calf,* and *sheep* from Saxon, and *beef, veal,* and *mutton* from Romance origin; as well as *alcatifa* 'carpet,' *aljava* 'quiver,' *quilate* 'carat,' *quintal* a 'kind of weight,' imported into Portuguese from the Arabic القطيفة ا الجعبة ا قراط and قنطر.

From the above analysis of Koṅkaṇî it results, that the elements entering into its composition are mainly Sanskṛit; in a lesser proportion Drâviḍian, closely allied to Tulu and Kânarese; Persian; and lastly Portuguese. What language the aboriginal inhabitants spoke before the advent of the Âryan colonies, who might have come down in more than one stream, and at successive periods, it is now extremely difficult to say; nor can one feel justified in ascribing the Drâviḍian terms found in Koṅkaṇî to the original speech, for these might have been imported into that language at a later date, during the rule of the Kânarese sovereigns over the Koṅkaṇ. It may, however, be asserted without fear of contradiction, that the basis of the language, that is, the largest number of vocables, and its general construction is entirely Âryan, or descended from Sanskṛit.

To recapitulate then, it is evident that the Koṅkaṇî language is not that very slight dialectic difference which exists between the language of the Dakhaṇ and the corresponding country of the Koṅkaṇ, but is quite distinct from, though cognate with, Marâṭhî, with a predominance of Sanskṛit words and a faint Turanian or Drâviḍian element. It has an elaborate grammar of its own and a rich vocabulary, derived from different sources, all elements having now in course of time lost their autonomy, and become so fused together that only a careful analysis can discover their origin or etymology. All the components entering into its formation can be explained both by the geographical position of the language, being wedged into between two great and powerful families of languages in India, *viz.*, Âryan and Drâviḍian, and considerably influenced by an European language, which has had a longer period of existence here than any other Western tongue, and by the several political vicissitudes that country has undergone in the course of the last eight or ten centuries, besides the ethnological difference or relations of its inhabitants, which can be distinguished by the examination of the dialects, provincialisms and prosodiacal accentuations, peculiar to each class, from the *Farazes* to the *Senoys*, making up the population of the Koṅkaṇ.

It remains now to consider collectively the whole language by itself, and notice some of its general peculiarities, which segregate it from other Neo-Âryan tongues. It is generally believed that the language of mountaineers differs from that of the inhabitants of valleys and plains, the sounds of the former being rough and harsh, and of the latter soft and smooth. Contrary to this belief, Mr. Beames [1] thinks that Koṅkaṇî has, not unlike Bengâlî, a tendency to thicken and debase the pronunciation from their proximity to the sea and the low swampy nature of the country. These may be the peculiarities of Bengâlî, such as the anusvâra playing a very prominent part, preferring long *a* to the short one, श to स, ण to न, and retaining a final स in some terminations, in all of which points Bengâlî differs from Hindî. But these cannot be said to be the peculiarities of Koṅkaṇî, nor does the analogy between Bengâlî and Koṅkaṇî with regard to the inference to be drawn from their being spoken in the vicinity of the sea hold good, it being illogical to generalize from one or two instances. Sir H. Maine has discovered in another field a similar tendency to generalizations from particulars. He writes :—" Mr. Buckle, in the general introduction to his History of Civilization, has derived all the destructive institutions of India and the peculiarities of its people from their consumption of rice. From the fact, he tells us, that the exclusive food of the natives of India is of an oxygenous rather than of a carbonaceous character, it follows by an inevitable law that caste prevails, that oppression is ripe, that rents are high, and that custom and law are stereotyped. The passages ought to be a caution against over-bold generalization, for it unfortunately happens that the ordinary food of the people of India is not rice. It is a product of the coast, growing on the deltas of the great rivers, and only at one point of the country extending any distance inland."[2]

---

[1] *Op. Cit.* Vol. I. p. 104.

[2] *The Effects of Observation of India upon Modern Thought*, Calcutta 1875, p. 9-10.

Not unlike the instance of rice, it just happens that Koṅkaṇî, in spite of its proximity to the sea, differs unfortunately from Bengâlî in the peculiarities abovementioned. The anusvâra is not more heard in the Koṅkaṇ than in the Dakhaṇ. If one talks Koṅkaṇî through the nose, it is a personal defect, not one of the language. Then Koṅkaṇî prefers short *a* to long *a*, and *o* to *a*, स to श and न to ण, and rejects a final स in most of its terminations. It is altogether a soft and smooth language. Dr. Murray Mitchell[1] has remarked, with regard to this theory of phonetic changes being based on difference of climate, that it is an unsound one. Although an interesting inquiry, that of the effect of climate on pronunciation, and one well deserving attention, the explanation offered, he says, cannot be accepted, as he does not think that the pronunciation in the Koṅkaṇ is thickened or debased, when compared with that of the Dakhaṇ. "As for nasal sounds," he adds, "they abound in French and are rare in Italian; and we have been in the habit of ascribing their prevalence in the former to the Celtic, which was the old speech of Gaul. In so far as proximity to the sea has an influence, Italia nought to be more nasal than French. Then as to *s* and *ś*. Take the famous instance of *shibboleth* and *sibboleth,* and the explanation falls. So does it, we apprehend, in many other cases. In spite of proximity to the sea, the inhabitants of Britain say *snow;* while in spite of distance from the sea, Southern as well as Northern Germany says *schnee*. Mr. Beames also mentions a tendency to use ण for न as showing the same effect in the Koṅkaṇ. Well, but all Mahârâshṭra makes the infinitive in णें, while in Hindî it is ना; and we cannot see how climate can account for the distinction. Besides, is it not the cerebral *ṇ* a stronger, manlier letter than the dental *n*?"

In conclusion, considering the Koṅkaṇî language synthetically, it may be asserted that it displays every affinity with Sanskṛit, not only in the possession of common roots, but also in the similarity of grammatical structure. The incidence of the language, the analysis of inflections, and even syllabic accentuation can all be directly traced to Sanskṛit. Vocables of a purely private or domestic character, such as those expressing the natural relations of parents, children and kindred generally, are descended from the same Âryan tongue. In short, the formative and symbolic portion of the language is of Sanskṛit origin, while the notional or presentive portion is of both Sanskṛit and other sources. Of these sources Persian contributes its quota of useful vocables relating to the military art, revenue administration and navigation; and Kânarese, terms of objective nature with a considerable amount of particles; while to Portuguese no distinct place can be assigned, on account of its incorporation into Koṅkaṇî being regulated more by caprice and ignorance than by any fixed law of the progress or development of languages. The negligence of the speaker is not seldom the cause of this indiscriminate mingling of Portuguese words in conversation where Koṅkaṇî equivalents are at hand. When synonyms from Sanskṛit and Kânarese sources occur, such as *phator* and *gundó* 'stone,' the former terms are, as a rule, used by the higher, and the

---

[1] The *Indian Antiquary,* Vol. IV. Bombay 1875, p. 187-188.

latter by the lower classes, whose pronunciation is, moreover, extremely thick and debased. Sometimes two apparently synonymous words, when derived from two different languages, bear diverse acceptations or meanings; thus these very words, *phator* and *gundó*, are used in different senses the former meaning large, and the latter small 'stones.'

II.

Passing on now to treat of Koṅkaṇî literature, I shall confine myself to such brief general statements as may afford a tolerably accurate view of the subject, without entering into details; although the materials at our disposal are far from scarce, to give a full and complete review of which would require at least a volume.

This subject might have been divided into two parts, *viz.*, works written by the natives of the Koṅkaṇ before the arrival of the Portuguese in India, and those written by the Portuguese missionaries and others subsequent to the conquest. But most unfortunately it so happens that of the former we have scarcely any remnant, although tradition current in the country ascribes to certain Koṅkaṇî Brâhmaṇs writings which were once extant, but which were destroyed by the Portuguese missionaries in their mistaken zeal to propagate Christianity. Documents of the early days of the conquest inform us how short-sighted and narrow-minded were those persons, whom the preservation of the ancient MS. and their study would have otherwise helped to produce more proselytes amongst the Koṅkaṇâs by preaching to them in their native tongue, instead of at a later date being obliged to make fresh attempts to write Koṅkaṇî grammars, which proved abortive, as will be shown hereafter, from the want of a vernacular basis on which to raise their superstructure.

The religious zeal or fanaticism, which blinded those missionaries for the moment to the usefulness of the works they destroyed, may well be excused, considering the character of the epoch. The history of mankind is already full of examples of how sectarian differences, bigotry, and superstition have deprived the world of literary treasures of considerable worth. The historian Vallerius Maximus, the contemporary of Patercolus, and often quoted by Pliny the Elder, Plutarch, Gallius, and others, tells us, in his *Exempli Memorabili* (lib. I. cap. 1), that some workmen having discovered in a stone chest seven Latin books of Pontifical laws, and seven Greek ones of philosophy, the former were preserved with great care, while the latter were burnt by the order of the Senate in the presence of the people, because they contained doctrines contrary to their national religion. Some centuries after we hear of the famous library of Alexandria being burnt by the Moslems amidst the religious enthusiasm and ardour for the triumph of the religion of Islâm, which work of incendiarism is stigmatized by Europeans as a piece of Vandalism, and its authors as barbarians, although the affair seems to be much exaggerated by the enemies of the Muhammadan religion. But this is not without its parallel in Europe itself. Seven centuries later the Spaniards, animated by the same spirit of bigotry and fanaticism, committed eighty thousand Arabic manuscripts to the flames in the public square of Granada. What the Spaniards did in Granada, the Portuguese imitated in Goa, only substituting Indian for Arabic manuscripts.

But it is not the blind zeal and ignorance of the early missionaries alone that has contributed to deprive us of the writings of the ancient Koṅkaṇî authors. As late as the last century there were priests gravely advising the Portuguese Government to abolish the Koṅkaṇî language, as if a language were a mere custom to be easily dealt with by a legislative enactment. I cannot, however, do better than translate here the following by the late J. H. da Cunha Rivara :—" In the first excitement of the conquest," he says, " the Hindû temples were destroyed, all the emblems of their worship were crumbled to dust, and all the books written in the vernacular language burnt, as convicted or suspected of containing the precepts and doctrine of idolatry. They intended also to exterminate all that part of the population which would not soon be converted : and this was their wish not then alone, but even two centuries after, when there was one person recommending with a magisterial gravity this measure to the Government.[1] But India was not America. If in this could the European conquerors exterminate in a short time the indigenous races, weak, and totally savage, and repeople the country with inhabitants imported from Europe ; the long distance at which is placed the Indian territory from the metropolis, and especially the invincible resistance, which was naturally offered by a numerous people, amongst whom the higher classes had attained an elevated degree of civilization, compelled the conquerors to avoid all open violence, and prefer indirect, though not mild, means, to obtain this end."[2]

From the very day the Portuguese formed settlements in India until the last century, or until the comparatively liberal policy of the great Minister of King D. José, Marquis of Pombal, was happily inaugurated in India, the Portuguese Government, through the advice of ecclesiastical authorities, not only withheld every kind of encouragement from the study of the Koṅkaṇî language and literature, or any other Indian vernacular, but promoted persecutions of all sorts. Goa was conquered in 1510, but we read of a bishop, as late as 1548, collecting Hindû works with the object of putting a stop to idolatry, which is a mere euphemism for consigning them to the flames.[3] And if any attempt was ever made to cultivate the language, the results did not become apparent at all until the next century, and this entirely on behalf of the spreading of Christianity.

In 1684, however, we are not a little surprised to see a viceregal proclamation forbidding the use of Koṅkaṇî, and insisting on the natives of the Koṅkaṇ speaking Portuguese. And the surprise is not lessened when one learns that so absurd a decree should have met with the approval of the king.[4] Later on still we find an Inquisitor of Goa writing in 1731 to the king thus :—" The first and

---

[1] *Liv. das Monções*, No. 94, fl. 121.
[2] *Gram. da Ling. Concani*, Nova-Goa 1857, p. XLIX.
[3] *Ibid* p. L. [4] *Ibid* p. LXXI.—II.

principal cause of this so lamentable a ruin (the perdition of souls) is the non-observance of the law of His Most Serene Lord Dom Sebastião, of glorious memory, and of the Goanese Councils, which forbids to the natives of the country to speak in their idiom, compelling them to speak only the Portuguese language."[1] One may give innumerable quotations like unto this from the writings of these ecclesiastics, which go far to prove the absolute neglect and decay of the study of the Koṅkaṇî language and literature; but what has been cited above is enough for the purpose.

We have, therefore, no materials at hand to treat of the Koṅkaṇî literature before the arrival of the Portuguese, for these were, through the spirit of intolerance and fanaticism of the early Portuguese in India, committed to the flames. Nor is there any profane literature in that language worth speaking of subsequent to the conquest. All we possess is what may be called religious or sacred literature, written by the missionaries and their pupils, who were almost all natives of Goa.

In treating thus of this literature, which is really copious, we must begin with the works of Thomas Stephens. I have already written at length on the life and works of this author in the *Instituto Vasco daGama*, published at New-Goa in 1873, vol. II., pp. 245 *et seq*, and in my paper read before the International Congress of Orientalists, held in Florence in September 1878, entitled, *Materials for the History of Oriental Studies amongst the Portuguese*, to be printed in the second volume of the *Atti* or *Transactions* of that Congress, which, I am informed, are now in the press. Stephens came to Goa on the 24th October 1579, and died there in 1619. I need not do here more than add the following extracts in Latin, relating to this missionary, from two interesting works by Cordara and by Alegambe to those already given. "P. Stephanus," he says, "natione Anglus, quem cum Thoma Pondo receptum in Societatem docuimus libro hujus historiæ primo, numerabat vitæ annos septuaginta, hujusque temporis majorem partem, annos scilicet quadraginta, excolendis Salsettarum novalibus perquam utiliter impenderet. Gentis linguam, quam Canarinam vocant, adeo callebat, ut ejus artem conscripserit. Cum vero prodesse quampluribus vellet, at Indicam quoque linguam, quæ nobilibus in usu est (Indostanam appellant), adjecit animum, ediditque ea lingua libros de Christiana fide, non minus rerum magnitudine, quam sermonis elegantia laudatos. Obedientiæ cultor eximius, moderatorum imperia omnia pari excipiebat alacritate, nemquam auditus aliquid malle, quam quod jubebatur. Nec vero prius obediendi finem, quam vivendi fecit. In ipso supremo morbo, cum cibum ex toto fastidiret, contumaciam stomachi nauseantis vincebat, non vivendi cupiditate, sed studio obtemperandi: utque audierat vocem medici, vel præpositi cibum sumere praecipientis, quidquid fuisset appositum, invitalicet, ac repugnante natura, admittebat. Incidit ejus obitus, nescio quo casu, Goæ. At Salsettani ut rescivere mor-

---

[1] *Ibid* p. C.

tuum, eidem tanquam parenti suo funus honorificentissimum, non tam pompæ apparatu, quam copia lacrymarum celebraverunt."[1]

Alegambe writes:—"Thomas Stephanus de Bubsten, natione Anglus, Diocesis Sarisburiensis, vir spiritu Apostolico plenus, cum ab hero suo Thoma Poundo Romam missus esset, ut societatem tum sibi, tum hero impetraret, in eam ingressus est anno MDLXXVI ætatis XXVI. Absolutis philosophiæ studiis, peculiari quodam divinæ vocationis modo videtur ad Indorum salutem fuisse destinatus: nam per quietem exhibitum est illi domicilii quoddam, ad cujus invitabatur procurationem; quód cùm omnibus ritè partibus contemplatus esset, profectus postmodùm in Indiam anno MDLXXVIII deprehendit illud ipsum fuisse domicilium Salsetanum nostrum, quod primò illi incolendum, post etiam toto quinquennio regendum est datum. Salsetanam ille vineam totos XL annos excoluit, tanto suo solatio, Christianorum processu, Nostrorum exemplo, ut nec ipse tentaverit inde abscedere, nec eum alió transferre Superiores sint ausi. Primus canarinum idioma in regulas, ordinemque digessit. Industanum etiam, quo nobiliores utuntur, perfectè calluit. Magnâ mansuetudinis, humilitatis, atque imprimis obedientiæ laude floruit. Ejus vitam ardentissimis votis a Deo petebant Salsetani, qui eum ut amantissimum parentem diligebant, ut sanctissimum Apostolum (sic illi vocabant) venerabantur. Obiit Goæ anno salutis MDCXIX ætatis LXX formatus jam olim ab anno MDLXXXIX. Coadjutor spiritualis. Scripsit

Grammaticam Linguæ Canarinæ, cujus in India Orientali usus est.

Doctrinam christianam, Indicâ etiam linguâ.

Opus magnum, cui *Parana* titulus est idiomate Indostano, *in quo præcipua fidei Mysteria metro exponit*; quod tanto plausu exceptum fuit, ut Dominicis, Festisque Diebus in templis à Sacro prælegatur, magnâ omnium approbatione et voluptate."[2]

The works of Thomas Stephens are a grammar of the Konkaṇî language, a poem called *Purâṇa* and a Christian catechism. The first is a poor production, in spite of the additions made to it by Diogo Ribeiro, of whom more hereafter, and of the revision by Estevam da Cruz under the direction of, among others, the Provincial of the order Manoel Barradas, commissioned by the Præpositus General Mutius Viteleschi. Its only merit is bibliographical—an interesting relic of the times, and an early work of its kind. One may judge of its value or usefulness as a grammar from the following declension of the noun *ritu* 'custom':—

---

[1] *Hist. Soc. Jesu.* Pars Sexta. Tomus Prior, in anno 1616, Societatis 77, auctor Julius Cordara, S. J. Sacerdos. Roma, Anno Jubilæi 1750, P. VI. Liv. IV. p. 205. Father Stephens died in 1619, because, referring to that year at page 205, the author says that in that year three worthy Fathers died, *viz.*, Manuel Pinheiro, Thomas Stephens, and Sebastião Gonsalves. The first, who was a colleague of Jeronimo Xavier in the mission of Âgra with the Moghul Emperor Jahângir, died at Goa on the 13th August 1619, at the age of 66. The third, who was born in the diocese of Braga, is said to have died at Goa, at the age of 63, on the 10th of April 1616 from an epidemic disease, probably cholera, which prevailed at Goa and the adjacent country in that year.

[2] *Bibliotheca Soc. Jesu.* p. 437, col. 2.

Singular.			Plural.		
Nom.	*Ritu*	Custom.	Nom.	*Ritu*	Customs.
Gen.	*Ritu*		Gen.	*Ritū*	
Dat.	*Ritu*		Dat.	*Ritu*	
Acc.	*Ritu*		Acc.	*Ritū*	
Voc.	*Ritu*		Voc.	*Ritu*	
Abl.	*Ritu*		Abl.	*Ritū*	

Now following this paradigm, which is more applicable to the Latin and Romance languages than to the Neo-Âryan tongues, and preserving even the last vowel, which is generally silent, the word being pronounced *rit*, the declension of the noun ought to run thus :—

Singular.	Plural.
Nom. *Ritu.*	Nom. *Ritî.*
Gen. *Ritucho, chi, chem.*	Gen. *Ritîcho, chi, chem.*
Dat. *Rituku.*	Dat. *Ritîku.*
Acc. *Ritu* or *Rituku.*	Acc. *Ritî* or *Ritîku.*
Voc. *Ritu.*	Voc. *Ritî.*
Abl. *Ritun, Ritur.*	Abl. *Ritîn, Ritîr.*

He who reads Stephens's example would certainly take the word to be indeclinable. In the declined form the ablative case includes both the instrumental and locative. The genitive has all the three genders. Then Stephens's conjugation of verbs is just as faulty as his declension of nouns, and the grammar is altogether useless for the purpose of learning Koṅkaṇî. Perhaps it might have helped to learn the Koṅkaṇî of the Purâṇas, to be mentioned hereafter, but even this supposition is extremely doubtful.

Stephens's *Purâṇa* has more interest in it as a specimen of classical Koṅkaṇî, which, it seems, was once spoken, but became in time confined to sacred or religious purposes. The Koṅkaṇî now spoken differs considerably from that used even at the present day by priests in their sermons. It appears to be an intermediate stage between the Purâṇic and the current language. On this ground one may divide Koṅkaṇî into those two dialects into which have, from time immemorial, been split up the more ancient tongues, *viz.*, hieratic and demotic, the former employed in worship, and the latter in the common speech of the people. Stephens's Koṅkaṇî of the Purâṇa is entirely hieratic. This work is entitled *Discurso sobre a vinda de Jesu-Christo Nosso Salvador ao Mundo,* dividido em dous Tratados, pelo Padre Thomaz Estevão, Inglez, da Companhia de Jesu. Impresso em Rachol com licença da Santa Inquisição, e Ordinario no Collegio de Todos os Santos da Companhia de Jesu. Anno 1616.[1]

[1] "Discourse on the coming of Jesus Christ our Saviour to the world, divided into two Treatises, by Father Thomas Stephens, Englishman, of the Company of Jesus. Printed at Rachol with the permission of the Holy Inquisition and Ordinary in the College of all Saints of the Company of Jesus, the year 1616." The College of all Saints is the same as "St. Ignatius College" of Rachol, thus called from its being inaugurated on the vespers of the day of all Saints. It is also called "D. Sebastian College," from its being erected during his reign, and mostly at his expense.

This Konkaṇî Christian Purâṇa has always had a great demand amongst the lower classes of the Native Christians of the Konkaṇ. While the Konkaṇî grammar of this author, who calls it *Arte da lingua Canarim* (or Art of the Kânarese Language), has had only two editions, *viz.*, that of 1649, printed at Rachol in the St. Ignatius College, and 1857, printed at New-Goa, the Purâṇa has had three. In spite of this, the work is very rare, and is better known by its MS. copies than by the printed text. It is a selection from the Bible, or rather an abridgement of the New Testament, accompanied by explanatory remarks on the subject of the incarnation, passion, and resurrection of the Saviour.

This work is said to have originally been written in Portuguese and then translated into Konkaṇî. The translation was completed in 1614, as testified to by the Rev. Paulo Mascarenhas on the 3rd of April 1614, and the book was printed for the first time in 1616, as declared in the Colophon above given. It was dedicated to D. Fr. Christovão de Lisboa, Archbishop of Goa, Primate of India, &c., the dedication being dated, from the College of Rachol, the 29th of April 1616.

It bears amongst *licences* from ecclesiastical authorities, which precede the work, the *imprimatur* from Father Francisco Vieira, Provincial of the Society of Jesus, dated the 22nd June 1615, through the command of the Præpositus General, the very Rev. Claudius Aquaviva. The second edition was undertaken in 1646 under the auspices of Fr. Gaspar de S. Miguel, of the order of St. Francis d'Assisi, who revised the work with some other ecclesiastics on the 20th of February 1647, and published in 1649. The place where this second edition was printed is unknown. The third edition bears the following Colophon:—"Em Goa com licença da Santa Inquisição e Ordinario no Collegio de S. Paulo novo da Companhia de Jesu. Anno de 1654;" or 'in Goa with permission of the Holy Inquisition and Ordinary in the College of St. Paul the new of the Company of Jesus. Year of 1654.' The licences for this edition are signed by the Rev. Fr. Lucas da Cruz and others, being dated the 2nd of January 1653 and 22nd June 1654. From the time of the publication of the second edition this work began to bear the designation of Christian *Purâṇa*, a strange medley of Catholic and Hindû epithets.

This Purâṇa, as it is now found, containing, besides the text, licences from ecclesiastical authorities, the dedication, and an introduction in prose and verse, in praise of the author, by Fr. Gaspar de S. Miguel, consisting of fourteen strophes, published for the first time along with the second edition of 1649, is divided into two treatises, each of them called Purâṇa. The first part consists of 36 cantos, and the second, which is again sub-divided into four sections, of 59 cantos. The whole work contains 11,018 strophes, of which 4296 belong to the first, and 6722 to the second Purâṇa. Latterly, Fr. Pascoal Gomes de Faria, a native of Goa, added in 1722 some 237 strophes to the seven cantos from 45 to 51 of the second part.

This work is written in the *Ovî* metre, a particular measure in which stanzas of Prâkrit verses, such as the airs of Muktešvar, and the *Dnyanešvarî*, a paraphrase in Marâṭhî of the Bhagavad-Gîtâ by Dnyânobâ, are written. It is held in great esteem, as above said, by the lower classes of the Roman Catholics in the Koṅkaṇ. It was read until lately at a superstitious ceremony called *soṭî, i. e., shasṭî-pûjan*, a night-watch kept on the sixth day after a child's birth, to guard it against the influence of evil spirits, which they supposed were specially prone to attack them on that day. This fatalistic doctrine prevailed for some time even among some of the educated Portuguese families in India, as we are informed by an edict of the Inquisitors issued at Goa on the 14th of April 1736.

As a specimen of this Christian Purâṇa, two stanzas, which I have translated literally into English, are appended below, without, however, taking any liberty with the original orthography of the text.

Qhuda truna vŏrzuni Sitŏ usnŏ sahuni Deho danddo cŏruni Hŏta nitcŏ.	Contemning hunger and thirst, Bearing heat and cold, Striking the body, He was always.
Suamiache bhŏcti vanchoni Dugi vassŏna nahí mŏni Dheani mŏni ŏntŏcŏrnim Ecŏhi Devŏ.[1]	Besides the love of the Lord, Had no other thought in mind, Neither perception nor consciousness, But of God alone.

This is said in praise of St. John the Baptist.

The next work in Koṅkaṇî of Father Thomas Stephens is entitled "Doutrina Christã em Lingua Bramana-Canarim, ordenada á maneira de dialogo, para ensinar os meninos pelo Padre Thomaz Estevão, Jesuita, no Collegio de Rachol, 1622, 8° (Christian doctrine in the Brâhmaṇ-Kânarese language, arranged in dialogue to teach children, by the Fr. Thomas Stephens, Jesuit, in the College of Rachol, 1622). This work is supposed to be a translation into Koṅkaṇî from the Portuguese book called *Cartilha* of Padre Marcos Jorge, although generally known by the name of its reformer Padre Mestre Ignacio Martins. It is referred to by Padre Souza in his *Oriente Conquistado*, vol. I. p. 22, and in the Agiologio Lusitano, vol. I. p. 382, col. 1.

But these are not the only works written in Koṅkaṇî by Portuguese missionaries and others. Although the printed books are not so many as the manuscripts, which have hitherto been preserved, still they are, by their very nature of being accessible and circulated, better known and appreciated. The art of printing was introduced by the Portuguese into India as early as the middle of the XVIth century, the earliest publication known being a little book in Portuguese, entitled *Tratado da doutrina Christã*, or 'treatise of the Christian doctrine,' Goa 1557, whose authorship is attributed to St. Francis Xavier. There is ample evidence to show that they printed a considerable number of works, and some of large size, in several

[1] Purana II. Canto 18, st. 2-3.

languages, but of these latter very few specimens have been preserved. They even cut Indian types, the earliest being Tamil characters, by Padre João de Faria, a distinguished engineer, who designed in 1580 those gigantic arches of the ancient Church of St. Paul, which eventually gave it the designation of *S. Paulo dos Arcos* or 'St. Paul of the Arches.' But the largest number of works was printed in the Roman character, although from not knowing the etymology of words, from their ignorance of Sanskṛit and other ancient Indian tongues, and not having any conventional system to regulate the phonetic value of letters for their application to Indian vernaculars, each writer interpreted the sound by his own method of transcription, thus giving rise to a confused and often capricious mode of transliteration or romanization. But as far as the apprehension of sounds by each writer was based on the Portuguese pronunciation of the alphabet, which differs but little from the Italian one, it appears to have been in most cases satisfactory, and in some respects even accurate and complete.

As it is not the aim of this paper to mention here all the works published in Indian vernaculars by the Portuguese in India, a detailed list of which has already been given in my before-mentioned memoir on the *Materials for the History of Oriental Studies amongst the Portuguese*, with an account of the introduction of the art of printing in India, only the works in Koṅkaṇî will here be mentioned, first the printed, besides those of Father Stephens, above referred to, and then the manuscript or inedited ones.

To enumerate then the series of Koṅkaṇî works and their authors in chronological order, the first we meet with are those by Padre Diogo Ribeiro. One of his writings bears the following heading:—"Declaraçam da Doutrina Christam collegida do cardeal Roberto Bellarmino da companhia de Jesu e outros autores. Composta em lingua Bramana vulgar pello Padre Diogo Ribeiro da mesma companhia, portugues natural de Lisboa. Impresso no collegio de Sancto Ignacio da Companhia de Jesu em Rachol. Anno de 1632." 4to, pp. VII-105. A copy of this work with some of the early works printed at Goa were exhibited at the Portuguese section of the *Exposition Universelle de Paris* in 1867.[1]

This writer is said to have made some additions to the Koṅkaṇî Grammar by Father Stephens, and to a vocabulary of Koṅkaṇî and Portuguese and *vice versâ*, originally written by nine Fathers of the Society, a few MS. copies of which are still extant, in the year 1626, "with various modes of speaking." It is said, moreover, that this writer translated the *Vidas dos Santos* into Koṅkaṇî and had the book printed *typis collegii Goani*. But no copy of this work exists at present.

Then follows in chronological order the book entitled:—Discurso sobre a vida do Apostolo S. Pedro, em que se refutam os principaes

---

1 I myself saw this work at that time in Paris, but a correct list of all the works thus exhibited will be found in the interesting *brochure* of Mr. I. Gracias, entitled *A Imprensa em Goa*, published last year at New-Goa.

erros do Oriente, compostos em verso em lingua bramana marasta pelo Padre Estevão da Cruz, Goa—Bom Jesus—1634, vol. II. fol.

The next author is Padre Antonio de Saldanha, who wrote the following Koṅkaṇî works under the following headings :—"*Archaryevanta Bragta Santo Antoniche* ou Tratado dos Miligres, que pelos merecimentos do glorioso St. Antonio, assim em vida do Santo, como depois de sua morte, foi nosso Senhor servido obrar : como a vida do mesmo Santo ; traduzido e composto na Lingua da terra corrente para serem de todos mais facilmente entendido, pelo Padre Antonio de Saldanha da Companhia de Jesus, natural de Marrocos. No collegio de Rachol, 1655." 4to.

"Rosas e boninas deleitosas do ameno Rozal de Maria e seu Rozario, traduzido e composto com proveitosos Moraes para bem das almas. Rachol." 4to. No date.

"Fructo da Arvore da Vida a nossas almas e corpos salutifero, illustrado com varios Moraes para proveito das almas e honra de Nosso Senhor Jesus Christo. Rachol." 4to. There is also no date.

Both the above works bear, as above said, no date of publication. They must have been printed between the years 1615 and 1663, these being the years in which he entered the Society and of his death, which took place at Rachol. He also wrote the following works, but were not printed :—

"Vocabulario da Lingua Concanica."
"Beneficios insignes dos Anjos Custodios."
"Baculo pastoral para administração dos Sacramentos e mais obrigações parochiaes." fol.

Then follows Padre Miguel d'Almeida, who wrote :—"Jardim dos Pastores ou Festas do anno na lingua Brahmina. Livro doutrinal. Goa no collegio da Companhia, 1658" 8vo. An extract from this work is given by the late P. N. Pires in his *Grammatica Maratha*. It is a panegyric of St. Lawrence, of which here is a specimen :—"Hê ituleí prataqhepanni amanchea mugtiunta Bhagta Sam Lourençã tthai barê drustty paddalê, zaca Deuana vdhandda manuppada pailo, tachhé nãua rupa, quirti, mahima, sagallea saunssaraca phancaily, quitea tanné Devachy seua bhagti carun, tache' xastra sumurti vpadessa sambhallileti, va tache' chita zoddile' deqhuun. Hea Bhagtane Deuachy yedy vhaddy seua bhagti quely, quy apule ballapani' leguma, nitecala Deuatempla Igrazantu zilo : Deuache seue bhagty nimity apuly cuddy, atmo, chita, mana, antascarana, Deuaca samarpile', zituli misã tiye Igrazantu sangati, ti itulii aica, va samesta' Sacerdotinche seua chacariyeca pava : São Xisto Srostu Sacredote zitule Bautissima cary, teãn ituleãi Bauptismõ lagui apanna hazira zai : ballalliquechea'ca Confessara caru'ca veta', pauitra vn'ção vharata', Sanctissimo Sacramento dita', sadha saruadha tache sangati vacha : yede vhaddy, va borauiye sicauanne nimiti, va aissalea' vtama' sagunna'chea abheassa prassagui, yedo vhaddu Bhagtu hounu vartalo, quy Deuache' xastra summurti sampurnapanni pallily, yeachi nhoe, panna tiche passauata apulo pranu dilo."[1] This is said to be the Koṅkaṇî spoken in Goa more than 200 years ago. But it seems to be the classical or rather the hieratic form of the language, in which the Purâṇas are written. If it was at all colloquial, he, who institutes a comparison between this Koṅkaṇî two centuries old with its modern representative, may well exclaim, *quam mutatus ab illo!* Such is, indeed, the transformation a language in the comparatively short period of two centuries undergoes even in autonomous states, which strive, with a view to their national dignity, to preserve the purity of their language by means of literature, arresting all changes, and stereotyping the forms inherited from a former age, that it is no wonder that Koṅkaṇî, an idiom of a small country, ruled by a foreign race, and without, at present at least, any aspiration to national independence, should within only a couple of centuries have assumed a form so entirely different from the old one.

The Koṅkaṇî of these Christian Purâṇas is, indeed, in relation to that used by priests in their sermons, which appears, as before remarked, to be an intermediate or transition stage, what the language, into which King Alfred of England is said to have translated the works of Bæda and of Osorius, is to that of Queen Anne's reign. Or, to indicate a parallel position in the Portuguese literature, what the Portuguese of the reign of King Affonso Henriques is to that of the poet Antonio Ferreira, whose style, unlike that of his eminent contemporary Sá de Miranda, is free from all those crabbed and antiquated forms, which abound in the latter, and is by unanimous consent constituted the legitimate parent of modern Portuguese; such is the Koṅkaṇî of the sermon above quoted to that spoken now-a-days.

It may be observed here *en passant* that the Purâṇic Koṅkaṇî is in reality a development of one of the Prâkṛits, or common colloquial speeches of ancient India, descended from Sanskṛit, and that, in spite of its being subjected, especially in the matter of phonesis, to alien influences, such as those of the Drâviḍian tongues of the neighbouring peoples, it is still a strictly Prâkṛitic language.

Amongst these Prâkṛits the western members of this Âryan group of languages are said to be older than the eastern ones. The earliest date generally ascribed to their formation is the seventh century, when the decay of Buddhism brought about not only great linguistic changes, but also a considerable number of currents and counter-currents of emigrations from place to place, amongst them probably holding a not uncommon place that of the Sârasvatas from Bengâl to the Koṅkaṇ. Those linguistic changes of that remarkable period

---

[1] *Op. Cit.* Bombay 1854, p. 105-6. The translation of the above is as follows:— "These virtues of the blessed Saint Lawrence were seen, and God had great regard for him, and caused his name, fame, and might to be spread throughout the world; for he served God well, and obeyed his law. He served God so well that from his infancy he used to go to Church, devoting his body, mind, soul and will to God to the extent of hearing all masses celebrated there, serving all ministers. He assisted St. Sistus, the high priest, in all baptisms, confessions, the holy sacrament administered by him, going out with him, and, through these means, great humbleness and submission, he became such a great saint, he devoted himself entirely to the propagation of the law of God, and in this service he gave up his soul."

at last laid the foundation of the modern Indian languages. And among these latter Koṅkaṇî, which is, of course, one of the western members, bears in antiquity and isolation close resemblance to Gujarâtî, which is not only an older form of Hindî, or more archaic dialect of that language, but an importation into the country by the Châlukya Râjputs. Not unlike Koṅkaṇî, which was introduced into the Koṅkaṇ by the Gauḍa Brâhmaṇs from Tirhut, and there preserved for some time isolated and cut off from the other dialects or members of the group, Gujarâtî was carried into the peninsula of Kâthiâvâḍ, and there gradually developed into a separate language, severed from all contact with the other Hindî dialects, retaining its antique forms, which have dropped out of use in the kindred tongues spoken in the neighbouring countries. And this analogy can be carried a little further when it is found on comparison that both Koṅkaṇî and Gujarâtî, notwithstanding all the phases of development and transformation they have undergone, owe the preservation of certain of their archaic forms, lost in the cognate neighbouring languages, to their evolution or course of changes being arrested by their isolation.

With regard to the remark above made of the rise of Prâkṛits from Sanskṛit, and the decay of forms derived from the latter, the mediæval Âryas may perhaps be likened in this respect to the French of the Merovingian period, when Latin case-endings were nearly dropt off, the people becoming careless about the peculiarities in the structure of their language. I say nearly dropt off, because they did not do away with them completely.

But to return to the Koṅkaṇî Bibliography; the next work of Padre D'Almeida is " Sinco Praticas sohe as palavras—*Exurgens Maria*—Goa. No Collegio da Companhia." No date.

"Sermoes de Santos, e do tempo quaresmal" vol. 2, 4to., MS.

This author is said, moreover, to have written a Dictionary of Koṅkaṇî, under the heading of " Diccionario da Lingua Concanica," which is said to be still extant in the manuscript form. But Southwell states that it was a mere translation of the " Thesouro da Lingua Portugueza" by Bento Pereira into Koṅkaṇî; while Barboza Machado in his *Bibliographia Lusitana* believes its first translator to have been Padre Diogo Ribeiro, who is said to have named it " Vocabulario da Lingua Canarina, com varios modos de fallar," to which Padre Miguel d'Almeida made some additions. Most probably the Dictionary—Portuguese-Koṅkaṇî and *vice versâ*—was a joint production of several Portuguese missionaries.

Two other voluminous works in Koṅkaṇî of a religious character, printed at Goa about the middle of the seventeenth century, require only a short notice here. The first is a *Purâṇa*, not unlike the one written by Father Stephens, but whose author is unknown. A copy of this work, *minus* the title page and some leaves, is preserved in the National Library of Goa. The other work is entitled *Soliloquios divinos*, by Father João de Pedrosa, printed at the New College of St. Paul in 1660, 4to, pp. 128. The preface of this work, in imitation probably of the invocation of Gaṇeśa, at the beginning of Hindû works, commences with the following rhapsody :—" Survai Pracarím vhõddi mugei Rannye Mariecõ nõmõscaru mõzo," which is an invocation of Virgin Mary in the style of *S'rî Gaṇeśâya-namaḥ !*

The other writers of the sixteenth century, who wrote several works in Koṅkaṇî on Christianity, some of which are still found in the manuscript form, are the Franciscan Fathers Amador de Sant' Anna, Domingos de S. Bernardino, D. Gaspar de S. Miguel, João de S. Mathias, Manoel Baptista, Manoel do Lado, and others.

Of the writers who composed grammars and vocabularies of Koṅkaṇî, which is by them called *Lingua Canarina* or *Bracmana*, there are several, such as Fr. Manoel Banha, who wrote a vocabulary, Fr. Christovão de Jesus, who wrote a grammar, although he does not appear to have published it, and others. But the most interesting amongst the works of this class are those written by two Brâhmaṇs, father and son, converted to Christianity, who had adopted along with a Christian name a Portuguese surname. These works, although written about the end of the seventeenth century, have not yet been printed, and their MS. copies are very scarce. They are entitled :—" Arte da Grammatica da Lingua Bracmana, disposta em 11 Livros. Obra mui necessaria para os Missionarios, Pregadores, Confessores, Compositores, Poetas, e Estudantes nas partes deste Oriente. Na Ilha de Chorão. Escripta por Estudante Simão Alz' (Alvares), Bragmane, Semnoye (S'aṇavî), Chorannense, etc. Anno 1694; and " Vocabulario de tres Linguas, Portugueza, Bracmana, e Castelhana. Obra mui necessaria para os Parochos, Missionarios, Confessores, Pregadores, Compositores, Poetas, Puranistas, e Estudantes deste Oriente. Na Ilha de Chorão. Escripto por Simão Alz' (Alvares), e seu Pai Lourenço Alz' (Alvares), Semnoyens (S'aṇavîs), Bracmanens, Chorannenses. Anno 1695." Both these works form together one volume, the Castilian part of the vocabulary being confined to the first page.

It has been said that these converted Brâhmaṇs were mere copyists and not authors of these books; but this is an unfounded supposition, especially when one considers the not small number of books these Goanese Brâhmaṇs, after their conversion to Christianity, and their being sent out of the country as missionaries to distant places, have brought to light. The *Congregados* or *Nerysts*, all of whom were Brâhmaṇs, were Christian missionaries in the province of Kâṇaḍa and the island of Ceylon, where they wrote several valuable works on Christianity in Tamil and Sinhalese languages, a list of which I have already given in the above-mentioned memoir on the Oriental Studies amongst the Portuguese.

It is a subject of no little confusion to foreigners, especially Englishmen, that there should be Brâhmaṇs with Portuguese names, and that some of these should be Christian missionaries. Many Englishmen on this side of India appear to believe that every one with a Portuguese name is a descendant pure or mixed from a Portuguese. There is no greater mistake than this, to expose which one must go back to the origin of the Portuguese conquest of Goa, and trace historically the influence it has exercised on the natives of the country. For every five descendants of the Portuguese there are ninety-five pure natives of Goa, who, on embracing Christianity, have adopted a Portuguese surname, been even enrolled amongst the Portuguese nobility, and acquired, in the course of time, the habits and customs of Western civilization; but they have remained still pure Indians, some of their high families being able to trace back their ascent genealogically for centuries to a period far anterior to the advent of the Portuguese in India, a state of things which not many noble houses in Portugal or England, or elsewhere in Europe can, perhaps, boast of.

The spread of Christianity in the Southern Koṅkaṇ was not a caste levelling process. It simply conciliated old prejudices with new privileges. A converted Brâhmaṇ became a Christian in faith alone, retaining all the social rights of Hinduism, and transmitting all caste prerogatives, untainted by any admixture of foreign or low-caste blood, through generations, to his present aristocratic posterity. The natives of Goa do not, unhappily, form a blend of races, as in Europe, where time may, perhaps, one day, weld all classes into homogeneity, but recognise practically as many tribes and castes as there are amongst those professing Brâhmaṇism. Until such a blending of castes takes place, it would merely be utopian to believe in the Indian *risorgimento*. One would be well advised if, until such a wished for consummation is effected, he could patiently stifle in his heart the cry of "India for the Indians," such as was once raised in the very centre of Goa in 1787.[1] Amongst these castes first comes the Brâhmaṇ of the S'aṇavî tribe of the northern lineage, then the Chardó or Vaiśya, the S'ûdra, and the aboriginal classes of Gauḍes, corresponding to the Âgraîs elsewhere, Kharvîs, Kuṇbîs, etc.

The people of Goa is altogether an agricultural one, only a portion of it migrating to other lands to serve in different capacities. It is from amongst the lower classes that are drawn those who betake themselves to domestic service. Nor are the Native Christians of Goa to be confounded with those of Bombay, the latter, although owning a Portuguese surname, being ethnologically of an entirely different stock, descended mostly from the Bhandharî and Kolî tribes of the Northern Koṅkaṇ. These are, moreover, British subjects, while the natives of Goa are Portuguese by nationality, enjoying all the privileges of citizenship since the establishment in Portugal of liberal institutions in 1833.

The caste rules among the Christian Goanese are not, however, observed with the same stringency as among their Hindû brethren. With the exception of marriage-ties, the caste has no influence in the least on social relations. All castes meet together, having due regard to rank or position in society, not unlike any of the advanced peoples of Europe, on one common level. They have given up all other insignia of Brâhmaṇic nobility, in which respect they form a not uninstructive contrast with the Native Christians of Southern India, especially Madhura, where De Nobili and his co-workers not only allowed them to wear, but went to the extent of

---

[1] *A conjuração de 1787 em Goa*, by J. H. da Cunha Rivara, New-Goa 1875.

wearing themselves, the *śendî* or the lock of hair on the crown of the head, *jânvem (yajñopavîta)* or 'the sacred thread,' and the wooden sandals. These were the Christian Missionaries, who came down to illumine the natives of India with European thought, but who became themselves imbued, so to speak, with Hinduism.

When De Nobili was called upon in 1618 to defend before the Synod of Goa the innovations introduced into Christianity with respect to what a historian of his society calls *linea, codumbus et sandalum*, he insisted on representing these as mere insignia of Brâhmaṇic nobility, adding that under a religious point of view, "mutare vestem nihil vetat, ubi agitur salus animarum."[1] This argument does not appear, however, to have satisfied the ecclesiastical authorities at Goa, who applied to the Pontifical Court for a solution of their difficulties. And when Pietro Della Valle was in Persia in 1620, he happened to come across, he tells us, the expedition carrying the report of this discussion to Rome.[2] The result of the affray seems on the whole to have been favourable to the views of De Nobili, the sacred thread being henceforward made to consist of three lines or cords in commemoration and honour of the Holy Trinity.[3] At a later date, or nearly eighty years after, a similar controversy appears to have broken out, but this time the affair was transferred from the Indian soil to that of the Celestial Empire, where Pinto and his companions were smuggling into Christianity Chinese rites, just as De Nobili had done with regard to the Brâhmaṇic ones.[4] On the former occasion the Christian Brâhmaṇs of Goa were appealed to and invited to express their opinion, but they abstained from voting on the ground of their ignoring the customs of the Madhura Brâhmaṇs.[5]

---

[1] *Hist. Soc. Jesu.* by J. Cordara, Rome 1750, Pt. VI. Lib. III. p. 168.

[2] *Viaggi.* Venetia, 1667, Pt. III. p. 85. About the life of this writer see the new work by the late Ignacio Ciampi, Rome 1880.

[3] *Storia dei Viaggiatori Italiani*, etc., by my noble friend Prof. A. De Gubernatis. Livorno 1875, pp. 31-32.

[4] *Chronista de Tissuari*, by J. H. da Cunha Rivara, New-Goa 1866, pp. 21 *et seq.* Cf. Hardwick's *Church History*.

[5] In the National Library of New-Goa is preserved a MS. entitled "Catecismo em q se—explicão—todas as verdades—Catholicas—Necesarias para a—Salvação—cõ exema ordem. Confutão—se tambem clarissimamente tódas—as Seitas gentilicas do Oriente—Obra verdadeiramente nascida pera converter—gentios—Composto—Em lingoa Tamul pello Veneravel P. Roberto Nobili da Compa de JESU—Fundad or da Missão de Madure. Traduzido em lingua Portugueza pello P. Balthazar da Costa da mesma Compa. Missionario da mesma Missão. Em obsequio dos Missionarios da India Oriental. Dedicado —Ao mui alto e mui Poderoso Sor. D. Affonso VI.—Rey de Portugal, etc. Anno de 1661.

This work is preceded by a biographical sketch of Robert de Nobili in Latin, and illustrated with a portrait of the missionary, clothed in the habit of a *Sannyâsin.* Robert De Nobili, called at Madura *Tatva Bodhayer*, was, on account of his costume perhaps, better known under the name of Roman Brâhman. A somewhat similar portrait of Constantine Joseph Beschi, who was known by the name of *Vira-mâmoni* and *Dhairya Nâtha Svâmi*, with a brief sketch of his life and writings by Mr. Pilley, is found in the Madras Jl. of Lit. and Science, Vol. XI. January-June 1840, p. 250.

His out-door dress was a long gown of light purple colour, with a waistband of the same colour, on head a white turban, in hand he carried a handkerchief and a long cane, his ears were adorned with a pair of pearl or ruby earrings, on his forefinger he wore a gold ring, and a pair of wooden slippers on his feet completed his dress. At home his costume was that worn by the Hindû devotees, and he abstained from the use of flesh, fish, &c. Beschi died at Manapar in 1742, and De Nobili at Mailapur, near Madras, on the 16th January 1656.

The Goanese Brâhmaṇs did not seemingly attach much importance to these insignia of nobility, except to those caste privileges which raised them above all other sections of their countrymen, to the extent of two of the religious orders in Goa, the Theatins and the Nerysts being constituted in their entirety of Brâhmaṇs alone, to the exclusion of all other classes. Their caste prejudices, if any, however, were no hindrance to their displaying zeal and self-denial in the propagation of Christianity among the heathen, and the country of Southern India from Kânaḍa to Ceylon, and from Masulipatam to the island of Madagascar are witnesses to the great exertions and devotedness with which these Christian-Brâhmaṇ Missionaries worked to spread the new religion they had adopted from the Portuguese amongst their brethren of South India, who still held aloof from the doctrines of the New Dispensation. Some of these Brâhmaṇ Missionaries were even raised to the Episcopate, such as D. Matheus de Castro, a native of the island of Divar, Bishop of Chrysopolis, D. Custodio de Pinho, a native of Verna, Bishop of Hierapolis, and others.[1] D. Matheus de Castro was the first Vicar Apostolic of Bombay and Puna, which vicariate was founded in 1660, and is now held, I believe, by a German.[2] It redounds, doubtless, to the credit of the Roman Catholic See that all races and nationalities should be thus invited to compete for her numerous hierarchical offices. That is, indeed, a practical illustration of the Christian brotherhood.

The statement regarding the elevation of Goanese Brâhmaṇs to the ranks of the dignitaries of the Roman Catholic Church suggests the idea of naming here those of the natives of Goa, who have for more than a century occupied exalted positions in Portugal and her colonies. They have, moreover, since the grant of the charter, or the establishment of constitutional government in the Portuguese kingdom, been elected to represent different constituencies in the National Parliament, as deputies to the Cortes, and been appointed to professorial chairs in the University of Coimbra and other educational establishments of the realm, besides holding high and honourable places in the military, naval, and civil service. But the subject requires a volume by itself, and being somewhat foreign to the matter under treatment, I have thought it more convenient to relegate to the Appendix **E** a short abstract on the Christian-Brâhmaṇ Missionaries from my memoir, read at the Oriental Congress of Florence.

But to return to the Koṅkaṇî literature. The following works, all of which have not yet been published, deserve to be here mentioned.

Preparação da Oração Mental, by Padre Pascoal Dias. This writer was a native priest of Goa, who also translated the *Stabat Mater*, and some other prayers and hymns from Latin and Portuguese. These

---

[1] *Noção de alguns filhos distinctos da India Portugueza*, by M. V. de Abreu. Goa 1874, p. 66, *et seq.* *Cf. Lingerings of Light in a Dark Land*, by Revd. Thomas Whitehouse, London 1873, p. 303.

[2] *Calendario Ecclesiastico*, by Revd. C. C. de Nazareth, New-Goa 1869, p. 270.

translations have been more than once printed at Goa and at Bombay during the last forty years.

But the works of an original character and of considerable literary merit, published during this century, are the Grammar and Dictionary of the Koṅkaṇî language, written by an Italian Missionary named Francis Xavier de Santa Anna, a bare-footed Carmelite, Vicar Apostolic at Verapoly, and published with emendations and additions by the late Mr. J. H. da Cunha Rivara. The grammar was printed at Goa in 1859, and the dictionary in 1868. This grammar, although superior in all respects to that of Father Stephens, is still far from answering the purpose of a complete grammar of the language; while the dictionary, which deserves better the name of a vocabulary, is a rather useful production. It is Portuguese and Koṅkaṇî, the verbs in the latter tongue being given in the first person of the present tense of the indicative mood, instead of the infinitive, *e. g.*, *fazer* 'to do' is explained as *caritã* 'I do' for *korum* or *korumku*, or according to the author's way of spelling *carum* or *carumco* 'to do.' This is the only vocabulary we possess in the printed form, and this boon we must be thankful for to the late Mr. Rivara, without whose exertions in giving it publicity, the work might have always remained a mere manuscript, obscure and incomplete.

There is another grammar of the Koṅkaṇî language, but it differs considerably from the above in being confined to the Koṅkaṇî dialect of the Marâṭhî. It is entitled *Grammatica da Lingua Concani no dialecto do Norte* or 'Grammar of the Koṅkaṇî Language in the dialect of the North.' This work was written by a Portuguese Missionary in the seventeenth century, and was for the first time published by the late Mr. Rivara at Goa in 1858.

As an appropriate companion to this grammar there is a *Purâṇa* written in this dialect by Padre Francisco Vaz de Guimarães, the first edition of which was published at Lisbon in 1659, the second at Bombay in 1845, and the third at the same place in 1876. An excellent bibliographical article on this writer and his works is found in the *Ensaio Historico da Lingua Concani*, by Mr. Rivara, published at Goa in 1858, pp. 172 *et seq.*, as well as an analytical exposition of his Purâṇa in the Journal of the Bombay Branch of the Royal Asiatic Society for 1851 by Dr. Murray Mitchell, under the heading of *Marâṭhî works composed by the Portuguese*, pp. 132 *et seq.*

Now with regard to the character used by the Goa Brâhmaṇs in writing the Koṅkaṇî language, the documents hitherto preserved in the archives of the village-communities indicate that they had not fixed upon one kind of letters. There were so many variations of caligraphy amongst these old dusty manuscripts, existing some fifty years ago, we are told, but most of which have now been irretrievably lost, that it is no easy task to classify them. Some of these papers were written in the old, and others in the new, Kânarese character; while there are some in the Devanâgarî, or popularly designated *Bâḷbodha* character, which literally means "teachable to children," with its cursive variety, known under the denomination of *Moḍi*, that is 'crooked or broken.' These two latter kinds of characters are now used by the Hindûs of the Konkaṇ in their epistolary and business transactions. A curious specimen of the former variety is found in the letter in the Konkaṇî language, before referred to, published in Van Rheede's *Hortus Indicus Malabaricus*, which I have reproduced in the Appendix, which also contains the Lord's prayer, the translation into Konkaṇî of the *Stabat Mater*, and two modern lyric pieces in Mongrel Luso-Konkaṇî verse.

With regard to the future of the Konkaṇî language, I need but make very few remarks. It is only an autonomous country that can preserve its language in a state of purity, and to its literature or rather to the learned men of that country is confided the task of rendering its forms classic and unalterable. But Goa has for centuries been swayed by foreign rulers, who have insisted on making their own the official language, or the language of the court, withdrawing at the same time all encouragement for the cultivation of the native tongue. Under these circumstances it is no wonder that it has been treated with neglect by the very children of the soil, and has, from the absence of a norma to regulate its forms, dwindled into the state of a jargon or *patois*. Add to this internal disorganization the power and vitality of the neighbouring tongues, and he need not be a prophet who foretells that in the course of a century or two the Konkaṇî language will be encroached upon by the Marâṭhî from the North, and the Kânarese from the South, a movement that has already begun, when Konkaṇî must succumb in the struggle. This has happened before, and it will happen again; for such is the fate of all weak tongues as of weak peoples.

Comparing for the nonce, and before we close this subject, the poetical compositions of the earlier date with those of more recent times one is struck with the decline, not merely in the form, but also in the ideal embodied in these macaronic verses, so to say, on account of the random admixture of Konkaṇî with Portuguese. He who reads or hears some of these modern *mandós* would certainly believe that the spirit of poetry had forsaken the place. But this is invariably the case where a country is in its decadence, or humiliated, depressed and degraded by despotism, or is swayed by a foreign rule, which, howsoever beneficial in material results it may be, does not, as a rule, manifest the least tendency to encourage the study of native poetry. In such conditions it is impossible for a great poet, even for a mediocre one, to arise. It is amidst the elements of national freedom and independence, and the pledges and evidences of former greatness of their country that poets grow up. How appropriate to the point, to compare great things with small ones, are the following remarks by Archbishop Trench on the literature of Spain. "For a great poet," says this writer, "without a great country, without a great people for him to be proud of, and which he feels shall in return be proud of him, without this action and re-action, never has been, and can never be. Elegant and even spirited lyrics, graceful idyls, comedies of social life, with all the small underwood of poetry, can very well exist, as they often have existed, and even thriven, where there is little or no national life or feeling; but the grander and sublimer forms of poetry, epos and tragedy and the loftier lyrics, can grow out of, and nourish themselves from, no other soil than that which a vigorous national life supplies."[1]

It will, however, be found, on closer examination of the poetical pieces of the earlier days of the Portuguese conquest of Goa until a century or more later, that they have preserved more of their vernacular purity, and retained their bold native rhyme in relation to the grotesque form of doggrel verses of the more recent times. The reason of this appears to be that a foreign nation or despotism cannot for two or three generations at least accomplish its work of destroying the mighty impulses of the free period of a people, demi-savage through it be, nor display, to quote once more the same writer, "its power in cramping, dwarfing, and ultimately crushing the faculties of a people. The nation lives for a while on what has been acquired in nobler, freer epochs of its life; and it is not till this is run through and worn out, till the generation which was reared in a better time has passed away, and also the generation which they have formed and moulded under the not yet extinct traditions of freedom, that the whole extent of the spiritual, moral, and intellectual mischief becomes apparent."[2]

What has hitherto been said refers to the form, external ornaments, in one word, to the style of this Koṅkaṇî literature. With regard to the subject matter, internal arrangement, or the ideal, whether moral or intellectual, of these writings, it has not been impossible for the foreign rulers to inoculate into the spirit of the natives of the country, which is religious by instinct, that form of faith and distinctions of kinds, which obtain especially among the Roman Catholic peoples of the Spanish peninsula, and have for some three centuries been embodied in the teachings of a certain order of ecclesiastics. It makes distinction between morality and religion, the latter being the object of all care, and not the former. This view has found its way into Koṅkaṇî literature, where the dogmatic side of Catholicism has been written upon to surfeit, but no writer has deigned hitherto to address two lines to the readers of this unique Christian Purânic literature on the duties of men, or moral obligations. This is a theme which gives a large scope for further remarks; but I must resist the temptation, as it must ultimately lead to the consideration of a subject quite foreign to the one under discussion.

I may, notwithstanding the extraneous character of these remarks, quote here, as *apropos*, the following words from M. F. Le Play with regard to the rise and fall of nations, and with them of their languages, "En résumé," he writes, "les peuples jouissent de leur libre arbitre : ils ne sont fatalement voués ni au bien ni au mal; et l'on ne saurait discerner dans l'histoire d'aucun d'eux une succession inévitable de jeunesse ou de progrès, de vieillesse ou de décadence. Quelque soit leur passé, ils restent maîtres de leur avenir. Ils peuvent toujours compter sur le succès, même après une longue période d'abaissement, s'ils reviennent à la pratique des lois morales. Au contraire, leur prosperité prend fin dès qu'ils laissent tomber ces lois en oubli."[3]

---

[1] *The Life and Genius of Calderon*, London 1880, p. 15-16. [2] *Ibid*, p. 12.
[3] *La Réforme Sociale en France*, etc. Tours, 1878. Tome I. p. 31.

APPENDIX A.

The following is the Testimonial in the Koṅkaṇî language and modified Devanâgarî characters, signed by three Brâhmaṇs, and published in the Preface to the first volume of *Hortus Indicus Malabaricus* by H. Van Rheede, Amsterdam edition of 1678, with its accompanying Latin translation.

स्वस्तिश्री शालिवाहन शाक १५९७ राक्षससंवत्सर चैत्र शुद्ध १० को
ची राज पाटणीं बैसिके रंगभट्ट तथा विनायकपंडित आपुभट्ट तेगै वैद्य
तानिं कोचिचा कुमंदोर आंद्रिकि फांद्रु त्यावगनिरोपान ह्या मलबारदेशा
नु आसिले ओषधमात्र वृक्षवालि झाडरवंड ओळखतेल्या मनुष्याकनु
स्तारोदस्तु तेते गांवांतु पेट्वून तिंतिं वारवद आणवून त्यात्या झाडांबें फस
फूल पान बीज सम स्तात्यान्यानुकाला वरिस पादून तिंतीं बितारिली त्याउप
रांत आमिं आमगेल्या वैद्यग्रंथाचानि घीटाजमाणी त्यांत्या ओषधाचे गुण
वाअरतु मतान जोजो गुण आमका कळेलो तो वात्यां आरवदांची नावं पळेउनु
आजि दानि वर्षं सकानि साजे आमिं लागिरावूनु दालिलु सपादून दिला तेल
टिक अविलाणुंचा कनज अगिविलणु आंमि आमचीनिसाणिकणु दिली
ते सत्यदाणुमानुवें जर इदस्लणु नागरबरपा नट्ट बरवून दिली श्री:

रंगभट्टु | विनायकपंडित | आपु वीआप

HOC EST.

AB anno millesimo quingentesimo nonagesimo septimo dicto á Bramanis *Palivanapaco* (qui apud nos est annus 1674) : usque ad decimum Aprilis anni dicti *Requeçao* (qui apud nos est Annus 1675). Ego Ranga Botto, Vinaique Pandito & Apu Botto, omnes tres de Natione & Religione Bramanas & Gymnosophistæ antiqui in districtu *Cochinensi* per mandatum Nobilis D. HENRICI á RHEEDE, Commendatoris terrarum Malabaricarum & Civitatis *Cochinensis*, curavimus per servos nostros qui notitiam arborum, plantarum, herbarum & convolvulorum habebant, eas ex terra Malabarica cum suis floribus, fructibus & seminibus ad Civitatem prædictam, ut delinearentur & describerentur, adferri, quarum nomina scripta sunt in libro nostro vocato *Manhaningattnám*, in quo etiam continentur virtutes & vires earum Medicinales, & præter hasce eis addidimus quod diuturna nostra experientia & magno labore ac sudore de iis didicimus & observavimus, & ut hic liber perficeretur, laboravimus per spatium duorum ferme annorum, ita ut omnis & quilibet, qui eum lecturus & visurus est, ei possit adhibere fidem quam ipse fuisset daturus, si res in ea scriptas ipsemet fuisset expertus; juramus itaque secundùm consuetudinem nostram, quod omne in eo contentum verum sit; in cujus rei fidem fecimus præsentes chartas quas propriis manibus nostris subscripsimus. Datum in Civitate *Cochinensi* vigesimo die Aprilis anni millesimi sexcentesimi septuagesimi quinti.

RANGA-BOTTO, VINAIQUE PANDITO,
APU BOTTO.

Traductum ex lingua Bramanum per subscriptum
VINAIQUE PANDITO
in linguam Lusitanicam, *& ex lingua* Lusitanica
in Latinam *per me*
CHRISTIANUM HERMAN de DONEP,
Secretarium Civilem Civitatis *Cochinensis*.

APPENDIX B.

The best prose piece in Koṅkaṇî is the Lord's prayer, which is also available for comparison with the other languages of its own and other groups. The Lord's prayer in Koṅkaṇî, published in the *Propaganda Fide's Oratio Dominica*, Rome 1870, along with other translations in 250 languages, at page 218, under the heading of *Oratio Dominica, Kanarice,* Dialecto Goana, is both grammatically and prosodiacally incorrect. I append below the prayer, as it is now said, in juxtaposition to its Latin equivalent, romanized according to the system in vogue amongst the majority of Orientalists.

The Lord's prayer is, indeed, far more suitable, as a standard of comparison, for translation into different languages than the Parables of the Sower, &c. (St. Matthew, xiii. 1—35); although the latter is seven times at least as long as the prayer. The parables were, moreover, translated into Koṅkaṇî, and published at Mangalore by the Basel Mission in 1872, this being the passage selected by H. H. Prince Bonaparte for giving specimens of the dialects of Europe.

Pater noster, qui es in cælis :	Âmchya Bapâ, tum sorgâr assai ;
Sanctificetur nomen tuum :	Tugem nam hoḍ zaum :
Adveniat regnum tuum :	Tugem râj amkam heum :
Fiat voluntas tua, sicut in cælo et in terra.	Tugî khośi zośi sorgâr zatâ tośi sounsârant zaum.
Panem nostrum quotidianum da nobis hodie :	Anim amchó dispoṭhó guirâs az amkâm dî :
Et dimitte nobis debita nostra,	Anim amchim pâtkam bogośi,
Sicut et nos dimittimus debitoribus nostris.	Zośi amim amcher chukleleamku bogośitaum.
Et ne nos inducas in tentationem.	Anim amkâm thauṇieṇ poḍum dium nakâ.
Sed libera nos a malo. Amen.	Puṇ amcher sorvoi vaiṭ vigṇ hetâ tem nivâr. Amen.

APPENDIX C.

Although a translation can never give an absolutely perfect idea of the beauty of the original, being generally a mutilation, or suggesting ever so much the meaning of some of those passages, almost unrivalled in deep and tender pathos, which may induce the reader to consult the original; still of the numerous translations of the *Stabat Mater* in several modern European languages, there is scarcely one to stand comparison for fidelity of sense or elegance of diction with the Koṅkaṇî translation of this sublime mediæval hymn of Giacomo Bendetti, or Jacoponus de Benedictis, as his Latin epitaph calls him. It is not only in Europe that this hymn has been set to music, where a series of distinguished composers and *maestros* from Josquim de Près in the fifteenth century, Palestrina in the sixteenth, Astorga and Pergolesi later on, until Rossini in our own days, have vied with each other to attach to it a melody with solemn elaborate richness, each drawing the inspiration for his music from the diverse surroundings of his life, as Astorga did from the scaffold, and Pergolesi from an execution and the intense grief of the survivor, writing it in an isolated spot at the foot of the Vesuvius, "with the shadow of death hovering over him." In Goa also this touching poem on "the sorrows of the mourning mother" has found, amongst the native composers, not a few who have embodied in song this cry of grief, expressed in melancholy rhythm, to be sung in Lent, it being now one of the favourite songs of the people. The Koṅkaṇî translation is by a Goanese priest by name Pascoal Dias, who is said to have flourished in the last century. It has since then undergone some changes, as the copies of the text evince considerable variations. The following is compiled from the collation of three distinct copies.

Stabat Mater dolorosa, Juxta cruxem lacrimosa, Dum pendebat Filius.	Aslî mâtâ dukhest, Cursachê mûlim chintest, Gedvam umkoutaló Putro.
Cujus animam gementem, Contristatam et dolentem, Pertransivit gladius.	Giechó otmó dukhamborit, Chintest anim dukhest, Dukhimchî boslî balî.
O' quam tristis et afflicta, Fuit illa benedicta, Mater Unigeniti!	Ah khitlî khont anim chintâ, Ti sodhevî bhoguitâ, Eklea-Putrachî mâtâ.
Quæ mœrebat, et dolebat, Pia mater dum videbat, Nati pœnas inclyti.	Ji rodó anim dukhó, Anim kampó gê vellê dekhó, Uttam-Putraché khôsṭ.
Quis est homo qui non fleret, Christi Matrem si videret, In tanto supplicio?	Kon tó munis roḍotó nam, Jesuchê Maieku poletanam, Itulé khosṭ bhôgtanam.
Quis non posset contristari, Christi Matrem contemplari, Dolentem cum Filio?	Kon dukhit nam zató, Zôr Christachê Maieku nyâltó, Dukhest Putrâ sovem.

Pro peccatis suæ gentis,
Vidit Jesum in tormentis,
Et flagellis subditum.

Aplê porgecheam pâpam pâsun,
Khosṭanṭ dekhló Putrâku,
Anim khaltó gerbhondanku.

Vidit suum dulcem natum,
Moriendo, desolatum,
Dum emisit spiritum.

Durlob Putrâku dekhló,
Pordeśi zaun mortaló,
Gedvam gîv sânḍiló.

Eia mater, fons amoris,
Me sentire vim doloris,
Fac, ut tecum lugeam.

Eh mayê, mogachî zorî,
Dî makâ dukh niborî,
Roḍumku tuge sorî.

Fac ut ardeat cor meum,
In amando Christum Deum,
Ut sibi complaceam.

Mogea kalzâku uzó mogachó,
Peṭoi, mogu korumku Jesuchó,
Anim sontósh Devachó.

Sancta Mater istud agas,
Cruxifixi fige plagas,
Cordi meo valide.

Sodhevî devachê mayê,
Ghâl tugea Putraché ghâye,
Mogea kalzâr.

Tui nati vulnerati,
Tam dignati pro me pati,
Pœnas mecum divide.

Tugea ghâyelelea Putraché,
Mogê passun meleleaché,
Khosṭ mogê sovem vânṭ.

Fac me tecum pie flere,
Cruxifixo condolere,
Donec ego vixero.

Tugea sangatâ roḍum śikoi,
Jesuchê dukhin makâ dukhoi,
Gîvont aum assom vêr.

Juxta crucem tecum stare,
Et me tibi sociare,
In planctu, desidero.

Cursachê mûlim sangat tuzó,
Anim vânṭ tugeam dukhimchó,
Sukh anim sontosh mozó.

Virgo virginum prœclara,
Mihi jam non sis amara,
Fac me tecum plangere.

Ankuarimchi ankuarî,
Nakâ zaum mogê thaim nisṭurî,
Dî makâ dukhamchi zorî.

Fac ut portem Christi mortem,
Passionis fac consortem,
Et plagas recolere.

Dî athou Jesuchea mornachó,
Dî bhag tagea khosṭamchó,
Dî ugrâs ghâyanchó.

Fac me plagis vulnerari,
Fac me cruce inebriari,
Et cruore Filii.

Vidâr mogî kuḍ ghâyan,
Kor dadośî cursan,
Anim Jesuchea rokhtan.

Flammis ne urar succensus,
Per te, virgo, sim defensus,
In die judicii.

Nivâr, mayê, sosnachó uzó,
Dîun dhîr anim adâr tuzó,
Hetoch dis zortechó.

Christe, cum sit hinc exire,
Da per Matrem me venire,
Ad palmam victoriæ.

Jesu, moger morn hetoch,
Dî mayêchó adâr,
Anvem paucheaku sorgâr.

Quando corpus morietur,
Fac ut animæ donetur,
Paradisi gloria. Amen.

Gê vellê morn het kuḍiku,
Lâgoshem kôr otmeanku,
Sorgâchem sosson sukh. Hośem zaum.

APPENDIX D.

Of the almost innumerable lyric compositions of the people in the Koṅkaṇî language a great many have been lost. And, for a few that have been saved from utter forgetfulness, the students of philology are indebted to Mr. M. V. d'Abreu, who has done for this popular poetry what the late Mr. J. H. da Cunha Rivara did for the grammars and a vocabulary of the language. I append below, extracted from his interesting periodical publication called *Ràmalhetinho*, printed at Goa in 1866, two specimens of these verses, the first in a dialogal form, and the second descriptive of the costume of a country-woman. I abstain from taking any liberty with the orthography of the text, in spite of his system of romanization being faulty and capricious. While drawing the attention of the reader to the doggrel rhyme of a bastard Koṅkaṇî, in which Portuguese words are freely mixed with the genuine vernacular ones, I must admit that there are other popular songs, in which the purity of the idiom is remarkably well preserved. Here follow the verses :

I.

Are cholie tum maca sang rê conali,
Anim aum ga choli malearcheam durgam bitorli.
Are cholie Malar durgant gór rê conalem,
Teveim goró tea muja avoi bapailem.
Are cholie avoi bapui con rê tugueló,
Aum nenom saibá, taca muntai João moteló.
João motelo to zobor amig mugueló.
Tum gorá vetorechi, tacá di recad zobreló,
Recad dileari tum macá.
Quitem rê ditolo.
Tuge paico mainco sanguno,
Tuge coré cazar zatoló.
Cazar zaucheaco aum baba meonam rê tuca,
Eca polquist estudantin utor dilam murê macá.
Utor dileari cholie caincho chintonam,
Tugea paico mainco songoleari diuchem raona.

pp. 55-56.

II.

Ague rendenim cati pagi, maram zali rati.
Matea dantonim bangarachi, bailo renderachi.
Fulá veló soró feniecho, gou rendenicho.
Goream sori pounreamchi, bailo renderachi.

pp. 7.

APPENDIX E.

A short extract from the abstract or summary of my *Materials for the History of Oriental Studies amongst the Portuguese*, read before the International Congress of Orientalists, held in Florence in the month of September 1878.

One of the most difficult and noble enterprises of the Portuguese in India was to convert to Christianity the high class Brâhmaṇs, and, when converted, to employ them as missionaries. There were even two religious orders of Theatins and Oratorians, originally introduced into Goa by Italian missionaries, into which only the converted Brâhmaṇs were admitted, to the exclusion of all other classes. These Brâhmaṇ-Christian missionaries soon won much distinction not only as zealous missionaries but also as writers. The Oratorians especially, who were appointed to the missions of the province of Kânaḍa and the island of Ceylon, wrote several works of considerable merit in Tamil and Sinhalese. Here is a short list out of a large number of their works :—

Peria Puranam or 'the History of the Bible', by Jacome Gonsalves.

Sinna Puranam or 'A Compendium' of the preceding work, by the same author.

Sugurta Darpanam or 'the Lives of Saints' by the same.

Devaprasâyen Tirrikkaduen or 'the History of the People of God' by Gabriel Pacheco.

The life of the Venerable Joseph Vaz was also written by the same author. But there is another biography of this celebrated Brâhmaṇ missionary, written by another Brâhmaṇ Oratorian, named Sebastião do Rego, in Portuguese, and admired by Portuguese scholars for the purity of his language and elegance of diction. The first edition of this work was published at Lisbon in 1744, and the second at Goa in 1867 under the able editorship of the late Mr. J. C. Barreto Miranda, who added several very useful notes to it.

Padre Joseph Vaz was a Brâhmaṇ and a missionary at Kânaḍa and Ceylon. When Cardinal de Tournon was sent as a Papal Legate to China, the latter offered him the bishopric of the island of Ceylon, which he declined to accept. Padre Vaz is said to have died in odour of sanctity, and his brother Oratorians of Venice even collected, we are told, his biographical notices in 1715, and obtained from the Pope permission to form the process of his canonization. The process was eventually sent to Rome during the pontificate of Benedict XIV., and must be lying somewhere amongst other documents in the archives of the Vatican.

The above-mentioned Padre Jacome Gonsalves was also a distinguished Brâhmaṇ Oratorian. M. Ferdinand Denis compares him in virtue and learning to the distinguished Bengâlî Brâhmaṇ Ram Mohun Roy, one of the reformers of Hinduism, who died in England, where he was settled some years before his death.

The Rev. Father Pacheco also wrote in Tamil the Life of St. Xavier; the *Gnyana Appam* or 'Pious Instruction'; *Alugai Kuravei* or 'Meditations on the griefs of the Blessed Virgin,' and some controversial works, such as *Satyajéyatten Sankuram*, in reply to the Rev. Mr. Mello, who was a Protestant Minister.

Two other works requiring notice here are the *Gnyana Pudhyel* or 'the Spiritual Treasure' by Sebastião Pereira, also a Brâhmaṇ Oratorian, and *Kristu Anusharam,* or 'the Imitation of Christ' a translation into Tamil from the Latin of Thomas à Kempis by the same Padre Pereira. Copies of these works have been preserved by the natives of Southern India in the manuscript form, but none of them appear hitherto to have been printed.[1]

---

[1] MS. p. 11. *Cf. Jl. of the Ceylon Branch* of the R. As. Soc. 1848, pp. 58 *et seq.*